GUITAR LICK FACTORY
BUILDING GREAT BLUES, ROCK & JAZZ LINES

By Jesse Gress

Backbeat
Books

San Francisco

Published by Backbeat Books
600 Harrison Street, San Francisco, CA 94107
www.backbeatbooks.com
email: books@musicplayer.com

An imprint of the Music Player Network
Publishers of Guitar Player, Bass Player, Keyboard, and other magazines
United Entertainment Media, Inc.
A CMP Information company

CMP
United Business Media

Distributed to the book trade in the US and Canada by
Publishers Group West, 1700 Fourth Street, Berkeley, CA 94710

Distributed to the music trade in the US and Canada by
Hal Leonard Publishing, P.O. Box 13819, Milwaukee, WI 53213

Text design and composition by Chris Ledgerwood
Music engraving by Elizabeth Ledgerwood
Cover design by Richard Leeds - bigwigdesign.com
Front dover and interior illustration by Mitch O'Connell

Library of Congress Cataloging-in-Publication Data

Gress, Jesse
    Guitar lick factory: building great blues, rock & jazz lines/by Jesse Gress.
        p. cm.
    ISBN 0-87930-734-X (alk. paper)
    1. Guitar—Instruction and study. 2. Blues (Music)—Instruction and study.
    3. Rock music—Instruction and study. 4. Jazz—Instruction and study. I. Title.

MT580.G723 2003
787.87'193164—dc21   2003040425

Printed in the United States of America

06 07 08   5 4 3

TABLE OF CONTENTS

Key to Notational Symbols v

Introduction vii

How to Use This Book ix

BLUES LICK FACTORY

   1. Blues Lick Factory Tour 1

   2. Three-Note Blues Licks 5

   3. Four-Note Blues Licks 23

   4. Five- and Six-Note Blues Licks 37

   5. One-Bar Blues Licks 49

   6. Extended Blues Lines 51

ROCK LICK FACTORY

   7. Rock Lick Factory Tour 59

   8. Early Rock 'n' Roll Licks 61

   9. One-Bar '60s and '70s Rock Licks 69

10. '60s and '70s Power-Trio Licks 75

11. Pentatonic Sequences and Speed Licks 81

12. Four-Note Contemporary Rock Licks and Modal Sequences 89

13. Contemporary Rock Speed Licks 97

JAZZ LICK FACTORY

14. Jazz Lick Factory Tour 103

15. Four-Note Swing and Bop Licks 105

16. One-Bar Swing and Bop Licks 117

17. Four-Note Jazz-Blues Licks 121

18. Extended Jazz-Blues Lines 129

For Mary Lou, Deidre, Doc, and Ginnie.

In memory of Ruth Arnold, Richard Taby, and Jay Kahn.

Special thanks to Liz and Chris Ledgerwood, Richard Johnston, Matt Kelsey, Nancy Tabor, Nina Lesovitz, Amy Miller, Rich Leeds, Tom Hassett, and Rich Maloof, and to Tony Levin for suggesting the title!

KEY TO NOTATIONAL SYMBOLS

The following symbols are used in *Guitar Lick Factory* to notate fingerings, techniques, and effects commonly used in guitar music. Certain symbols are found in either the tablature or the standard notation only, not both. For clarity, consult both systems.

HOW TABLATURE WORKS

The horizontal lines represent the guitar's strings, the top line standing for the high *E*. The numbers designate the frets to be played. For instance, a 2 positioned on the first line would mean play the 2nd fret on the first string (0 indicates an open string). Time values are indicated on the standard notation staff seen directly above the tablature. Special symbols and instructions appear between the standard and tablature staves. Fret-hand fingering is designated by small Arabic numerals below the tablature staff (1=first finger, 2=middle finger, 3=third finger, 4=little finger, t=thumb).

⊓ : **Pick downstroke**.

∨ : **Pick upstroke**.

Bend: Play the first note and bend to the pitch of the equivalent fret position shown in parentheses. Notes can also be pre-bent.

Reverse Bend: Bend the note to the specified pitch/fret position shown in parentheses, then release to the indicated pitch/fret.

Hammer-on: From lower to higher note(s). Individual notes may also be hammered.

Pull-off: From higher to lower note(s).

Slide: Play first note and slide up or down to the next pitch. If the notes are tied, pick only the first. If no tie is present, pick both.

A slide symbol before or after a single note indicates a slide to or from an undetermined pitch.

Finger vibrato.

Bar dips.

CHORD DIAGRAMS

In all chord diagrams, vertical lines represent the strings, and horizontal lines represent the frets. The following symbols are used:

——— Nut; indicates first position.

X   Muted string, or string not played.

○   Open string.

⌒   Barre (partial or full).

●   Placement of left-hand fingers.

III   Roman numerals indicate the fret at which a chord is located.

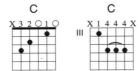

Arabic numerals indicate fret-hand fingering.

INTRODUCTION

For better or worse, we guitarists are essentially lick-oriented creatures—not exactly a desirable trait among musicians. After all, we're supposed to be thinking about things like melody, form, context, and the "big picture." But the truth can't be ignored. We all learn our melodic lines the same way: one lick at a time. And that's nothing to be ashamed of. In fact, there's nothing quite like the exhilarating feeling of ownership you get when you foster a new lick into your musical vocabulary. The Guitar Lick Factory was founded for those who recognize and embrace this simple fact of life.

What is a lick, anyway? For our purposes, it's a three- to six-note melodic fragment, or module. The Guitar Lick Factory is dedicated to providing its customers with a steady supply of fresh stylistic lick modules, interactively designed to link in almost any order.

Our production line begins with a hefty framework of blues licks, American-made and built to last. Next, the rock division fortifies the fleet with impervious metals. Finally, we detail the surface with luxurious jazz accoutrements.

Don't think that breaking down a musical style into a series of short licks decreases its value. These three-, four-, five-, and six-note modules are the building blocks that define the very essence of blues, rock, and jazz guitar vocabularies. By learning a genre's essential moves, you gain the confidence and ability to connect those moves into hundreds of longer personalized statements. And isn't that the name of the game? So get on line—the next Lick Factory tour starts now.

HOW TO USE THIS BOOK

For easy mixing and matching, The Guitar Lick Factory manufactures all of its licks in the keys of *A* major and *A* minor—a comfortable "middle ground" on the fingerboard. You can drop any of our licks into a designated major or minor barrel, pick out a few at random, and arrange them into longer lines. Of course, you should transpose all of the licks and lines in this book—as well as those of your own design— to all keys.

Rhythmically, we've notated our licks in as compact a manner as is practical. This makes them easy to read, retain, and combine, but unfortunately limits their diversity. To help you unlock their potential, every lick comes with an optional supply of rhythmic variations.

There are many ways to get from one note to the next on the guitar. The notational key on pages v and vi details how to interpret tablature and the symbols we use to depict techniques such as bends, hammer-ons, pull-offs, and slides.

At the Lick Factory, our Blues, Rock, and Jazz divisions often incorporate multiple tablature systems to illustrate identical licks played in different positions on different strings. Fret-hand fingering is notated below each tab staff. Occasionally you'll see a lick written in two different positions on the same tab staff, often with more than one fingering. You'll encounter two scenarios: two fingering variations that share one or more common notes, or two identical fingerings played on different strings (see examples on the following page).

The trick is to look at the upper line of tablature and fingering numbers for one lick, and the lower line for its fingering variation or duplicate. When only a single fingering appears, it applies to the lick in both positions.

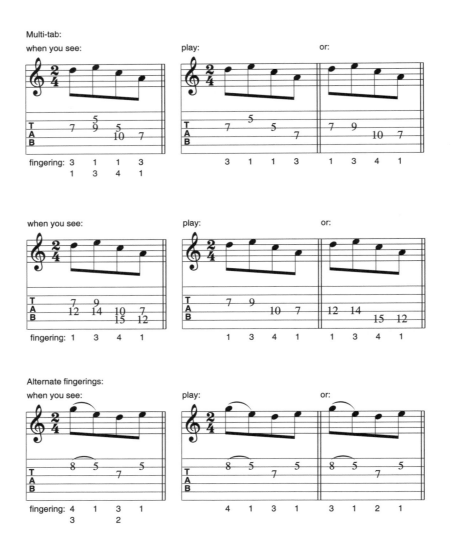

A bit of advice: Don't space out on the page! Because of the sheer mass of material presented, some pages can look intimidating. Stay focused on your goal: to get licks and lines off the paper and under your fingers as soon as possible. Work slowly and methodically on one lick at a time until you own it. (You'll find many music theory basics and prerequisites in *The Guitar Cookbook*, highly recommended as a companion reference volume.)

BLUES LICK FACTORY TOUR

Welcome to the Blues Lick Factory. We've got six departments here: four devoted to the production of three-, four-, five-, and six-note licks, and two that specialize in combining licks into longer lines. We take our work quite seriously. Many musical genres, including rock and jazz, are deeply rooted in the blues, and blues music is arguably the source of the "lick mentality" ingrained in most guitarists. And while it's not difficult to learn how to navigate a handful of licks through a 12-bar blues progression, transforming them into a convincing blues solo requires more than a cookie-cutter approach. To unlock any lick's true potential, you must learn how to manipulate it rhythmically, melodically, harmonically, and, ultimately, emotionally. This is the founding concept behind the entire Guitar Lick Factory, where you customize each lick to your own specs.

What's that? You'd like to work here? Well, why didn't you say so? Take an application. We'll finish the tour and go over a few prerequisites along the way.

Using only the highest-quality raw materials, our three-, four-, five-, and six-note facilities produce definitive blues-lick "modules" that incorporate many of the genre's inherent fret- and pick-hand techniques, including string bends, hammer-ons, pull-offs, and slides.

An understanding of basic rhythms and rhythmic subdivisions—especially slow 12/8 blues and medium 4/4 shuffle feels—will help users exploit these blues licks to their fullest potential. Each three-note lick is written as three eighth-notes in a bar of 3/8—essentially one-quarter, or one "beat" (dotted quarter-note), of a measure of 12/8. Count the notes "1-2-3" and repeat the lick four times to fill a bar of 12/8. Four-note licks are delivered as four eighth-notes in a bar of 2/4. Count these "1-and-2-and" and repeat each lick twice to form an entire bar of 4/4. Our five-note ("1-and-2-and-3") and six-note licks ("1-and-2-and-3-and") are also notated in 3/8.

One secret to creating an endless supply of blues licks is the ability to adapt any lick to any rhythm. Each three- and four-note lick comes supplied with a host of rhythmic variations to which any lick can be adapted. Additionally, any of these rhythms can be half-timed or double-timed. It sounds contradictory, but "half-time" means doubling the time value, or duration, of each note (half as fast), while "double-time" refers to halving the value of each note (twice as fast). It's also easy to combine 3/8 and 2/4 licks. In 2/4, simply treat each 3/8 lick as an eighth-note triplet, or convert it to an eighth-note and two 16th-notes.

Melodically, most blues licks use the pentatonic major, pentatonic minor, and blues scales. Though we've manufactured all of our licks in *A*, we've designed them to be playable in any key. Familiarize yourself with these scales and their fretboard patterns in all keys. Once you connect a lick to its host fretboard pattern, you can transpose it to any key by simply moving it up or down the neck to the appropriate position. Here are the grids for the *A* pentatonic major and minor and blues scales:

A Pentatonic Major Scale

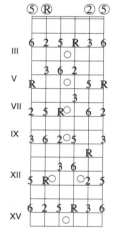
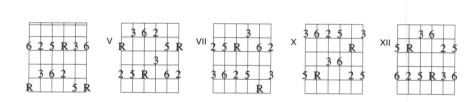

A Pentatonic Minor Scale

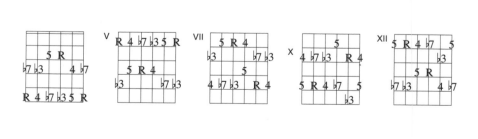

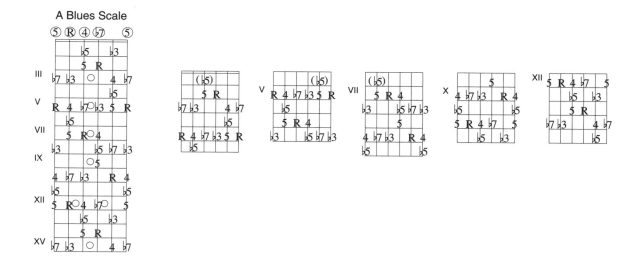

The 12-bar, I–IV–V-based progressions shown below provide the basic harmonic framework for most blues music. If you haven't already done so, memorize both progressions. The first is a "slow change" blues in A: four bars of the I (*A7*) chord, two bars of the IV (*D7*) chord, back to the I for two bars, two bars of the V (*E7*) chord, and two more bars of the I chord. The second is a "quick-change" blues in *A*, which adds more harmonic activity: a change to the IV chord in bar 2, the V and IV chords for one bar each in bars 9 and 10, and a busier I–IV–V "turnaround" in bars 11 and 12. Unless otherwise indicated, you can drop any lick into any part of these chord progressions.

Slow-change Blues

| 4/4 or 12/8 ‖: | A7 (I) | A7 (I) | A7 (I) | A7 (I) | D7 (IV) | D7 (IV) | A7 (I) | A7 (I) | E7 (V) | E7 (V) | A7 (I) | A7 (I) :‖ |

Quick-change Blues

| 4/4 or 12/8 ‖: | A7 (I) | D7 (IV) | A7 (I) | A7 (I) | D7 (IV) | D7 (IV) | A7 (I) | A7 (I) | E7 (V) | D7 (IV) | A7 (I) D7 (IV) | A7 (I) E7 (V) :‖ |

You'll need to know a few reliable I7, IV7, and V7 chord voicings to hear how these different harmonic settings affect each lick. You can also mix and match the 7th and 9th chords shown below:

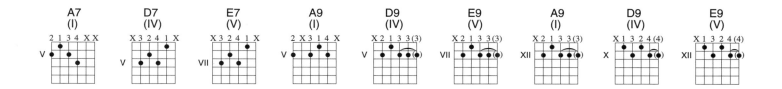

A few technique tips:

- Back up any bending finger with one or more additional fingers whenever possible. Generally, you'll bend strings 1 through 4 (high to low) toward the ceiling and strings 5 and 6 toward the floor.
- Add motion-inducing gradual quarter-step bends to $C\natural$ and $G\natural$ wherever they sound good. Learn to trust your instincts.
- You can add vibrato—an essential ingredient in blues guitar—to any note at your discretion. Think vocally and delay your vibrato slightly on sustained notes.

Your application looks fine and you seem eager to learn. Congratulations—you're hired! Report to the three-note Blues Lick Factory in the morning.

CHAPTER 2

THREE-NOTE BLUES LICKS

G ood morning—welcome to the Three-Note Blues Lick Factory. Now punch in and get to work! You'll be beta-testing every lick that comes off our production line. As mentioned during your tour, we decided that the most efficient way to manufacture and package these lick modules was to organize them into identical rhythmic groupings in a single key. Thus, each three-note *A* blues lick (grace notes don't count in the tally) has been consolidated into an eighth-note triplet. Notating them in 3/8—which comprises 25 percent of a measure of 12/8, the most common time signature for slow blues—eliminates the need for cluttered triplet indicators or brackets, and makes it easy for you to combine licks and adapt them to other three-note rhythms. With each lick we also include an Applications box, which reveals each note's intervallic relationship to the three primary chords in an *A* blues: *A7* (I), *D7* (IV), and *E7* (V). (If a given lick does not apply to any of these chords, the box is left blank.) The "Apps" box will help you understand at a glance why the sound of a lick changes over different chords. Grace notes and ornaments are included in the Apps box analysis.

Here's the drill:

1. The top row, or "a," examples illustrate the lick in three octaves. Choose one and play the lick as written until it becomes comfortable. (Hint: It's helpful to start with the second octave, which resides in the middle ground.) We've decorated each lick with a single ornament—a bend, slide, hammer-on, or pull-off. The multi-tab staves show how to play the same lick in up to five different fretboard positions. Investigate these and note any changes in the suggested fingering.

2. Memorize the lick. One key to retention is to repeat the lick until playing it becomes a reflex. Play each chord in the Applications box and develop your own ideas about which licks work best with which chords.

3. Explore the remaining two octaves. Again, note any fingering revisions or similarities.

4. Move down to the "b" examples. These present a trio of phrasing options for each "a" lick, notated in a single octave and laced with gobs of emotive "finger grease" (hammer-ons, pull-offs, and other ornaments). Rephrasing, which can range from subtle to drastic, is a great way to breathe new life into static, well-worn licks. Feel free to add or subtract ornaments as you see fit. We hope these will inspire your own "amazing phrasing" options.

5. The "c" examples alter one note in the original lick to produce one or more melodic variations, complete with additional Applications boxes. Try mating them with the original lick, and use them as jump-off points for your own creative variations.

6. Once you've taken ownership of a new lick, you'll be able to "hear" and "play" it away from your instrument. Feels good, doesn't it? Now it's time to adapt the lick to the rhythmic variations that border the bottom of each page. It's easy—just plug the notes of the original lick into the new rhythm. Memorize the rhythm first so you'll know when to play the notes. Some will work better than others; trust your ear and incorporate the ones that sound best into your musical vocabulary.

Follow this drill faithfully. By the end of your shift, I guarantee you'll know that lick—plus a dozen variations—inside out.

RHYTHMIC DISPLACEMENT AND MELODIC PERMUTATION

When it comes to customizing our standard line, these do-it-yourself tricks for rhythmic displacement and melodic permutation offer users more bang for the buck.

These licks sound fine as written, but every one of them begins on beat *one*. Try moving, or displacing, each "triplet" to a different downbeat in a measure of 12/8.

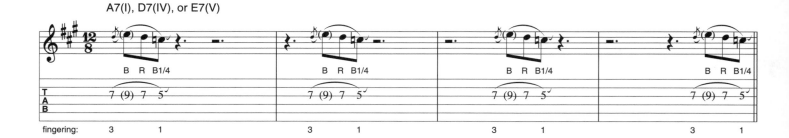

Three-Note Blues Licks

Most of our three-note licks work exceptionally well as pickup licks that begin on the final "beat" (last three eighth-notes) in a bar of 12/8. These sound best when you tack an appropriate chord tone onto the following downbeat.

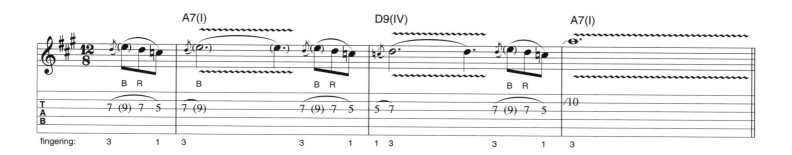

You can also play each lick starting on the second or third eighth-note of any beat in a measure of 12/8. Of course, all of these rhythmic displacements can be applied to any rhythmic variation.

Another great way to increase melodic mileage is to resequence the same three notes into every possible combination. Any group of three different notes will produce six (1x2x3) different combinations, or permutations—two starting on each note.

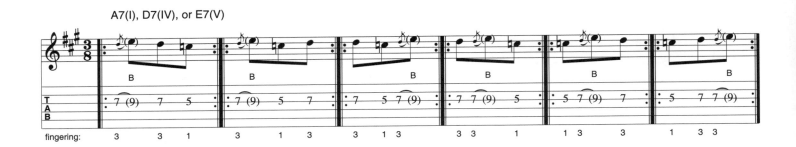

These permutations will also affect your phrasing options.

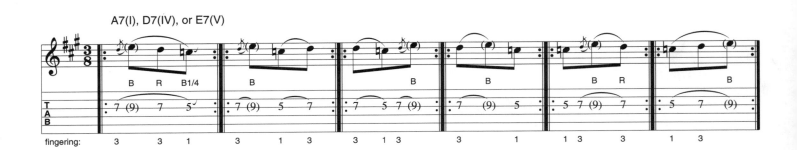

Got it? Good! Let's hit the assembly line.

Ex. 1a

Applications:			
A7(I)	5\4	b3	R
D7(IV)	2\R	b7	5
E7(V)	R\b7	b6	4

1b

1c

Applications:			
A7(I)	b5\4	b3	R
D7(IV)	b9\R	b7	5
E7(V)	7\b7	b6	4

Ex. 2a

Applications:			
A7(I)	4(5)	4	b3
D7(IV)	R(2)	R	b7
E7(V)	b7(R)	b7	b6

2b

2c

Applications:			
A7(I)	4(b5)	4	b3
D7(IV)	R(b9)	R	b7
E7(V)	b7(7)	b7	b6

Three-Note Blues Licks

Ex. 5a

Ex. 6a

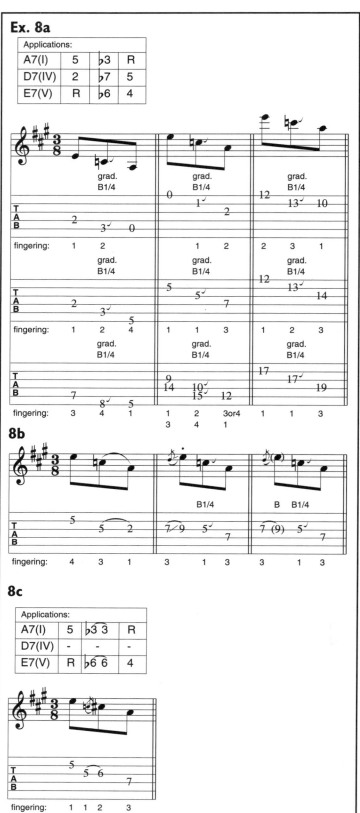

Ex. 9a

Applications:			
A7(I)	4	♭5	4 ♭3
D7(IV)	R	♭9	R ♭7
E7(V)	♭7 7	♭7	♭6

9b

*Pre-bend from 7th fret.

9c

Applications:			
A7(I)	4 ♭5	4	♭3 3
D7(IV)	-	-	-
E7(V)	-	-	-

Ex. 10a

Applications:			
A7(I)	♭5	5	♭7
D7(IV)	♭9	9	4
E7(V)	7	R	♯9

10b

*Pre-bend from 8th fret.

10c

Applications:			
A7(I)	♭5	5	♯9
D7(IV)	♭9	9	♭7
E7(V)	7	R	♭6

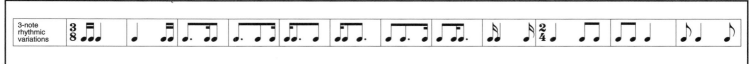

13

Ex. 11a

Applications:			
A7(I)	5	6	R
D7(IV)	2	3	5
E7(V)	R	2	4

11b

11c

Applications:			
A7(I)	♭6	6	R
D7(IV)	♭3	3	5
E7(V)	♭9	9	4

Ex. 12a

Applications:			
A7(I)	2	(3)	2	R
D7(IV)	-	-	-	
E7(V)	5	(6)	5	4

12b

12c

Applications:			
A7(I)	2	(♭3)	2	R
D7(IV)	6	(♭7)	6	5
E7(V)	5	(♭6)	5	4

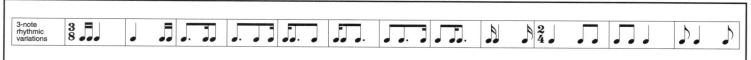

Ex. 17a

Applications:			
A7(I)	4	5	♭3 3
D7(IV)	-	-	-
E7(V)	♭7	R	♭6 6

17b

*Pre-bend from 7th fret.

17c

Applications:			
A7(I)	4	R	♭3
D7(IV)	R	2	♭7
E7(V)	♭7	R	♭6

Ex. 18a

Applications:			
A7(I)	4	(5)	♭7
D7(IV)	R	(2)	4
E7(V)	♭7	(R)	♭3

18b

18c

Applications:			
A7(I)	4	(5)	5
D7(IV)	R	(2)	2
E7(V)	♭7	(R)	R

Ex. 19a

Applications:			
A7(I)	4 (5)	5	♭7
D7(IV)	R (2)	2	4
E7(V)	♭7(R)	R	♭3

19b

19c

Applications:			
A7(I)	4 (♭5)	5	♭7
D7(IV)	R (♭9)	9	4
E7(V)	♭7 (7)	R	♭3

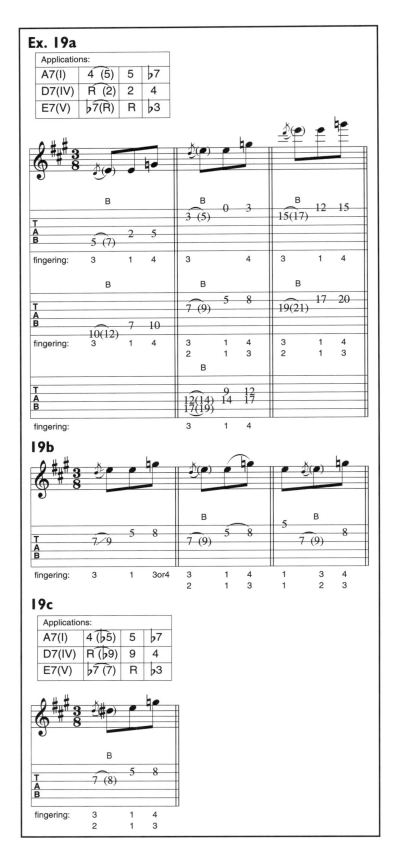

Ex. 20a

Applications:			
A7(I)	4 (5)	R
D7(IV)	R (2)	5
E7(V)	♭7 (R)	4

20b

20c

Applications:			
A7(I)	♭5 (5)	R
D7(IV)	♭9 (9)	5
E7(V)	7 (R)	4

Ex. 23a

Applications:			
A7(I)	4/5	♭7	R
D7(IV)	R/2	4	5
E7(V)	♭7/R	♭3	4

23b

23c

Applications:			
A7(I)	4/5	♭7	♯9
D7(IV)	R/2	4	♭7
E7(V)	♭7/R	♭3	♭6

Ex. 24a

Applications:			
A7(I)	5	R	/R
D7(IV)	2	5	/5
E7(V)	R	4	/4

24b

24c

Applications:			
A7(I)	5	R	/♯9
D7(IV)	9	5	/♭7
E7(V)	R	4	/♭6

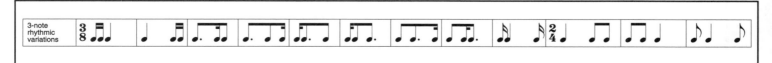

Ex. 25a

Applications:			
A7(I)	♭3	5	6
D7(IV)	♭7	2	3
E7(V)	♭6	R	2

25b

25c

Applications:			
A7(I)	♯9	5	6
D7(IV)	♭7	9	3
E7(V)	♭6	R	9

Ex. 26a

Applications:			
A7(I)	6	♭3	R
D7(IV)	3	♭7	5
E7(V)	2	♭6	4

26b

26c

Applications:			
A7(I)	6	R	♭3
D7(IV)	3	5	♭7
E7(V)	9	4	♭6

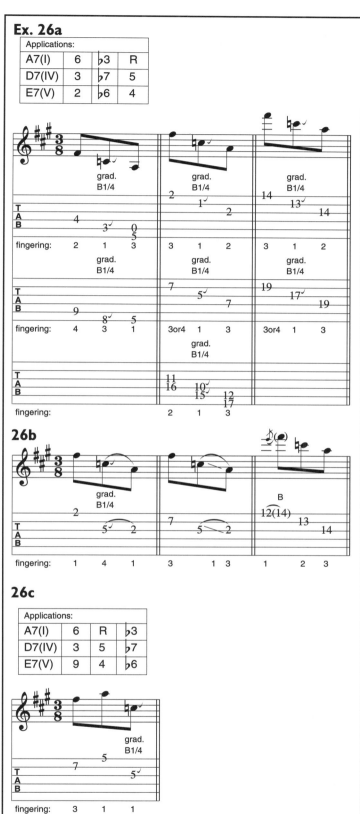

You've done well and deserve a promotion; report to the Four-Note Blues Lick Factory in the morning. And don't let those guys rattle you—some of them have been there for a long time!

CHAPTER 3

FOUR-NOTE BLUES LICKS

Hey, look who's here! It's our hotshot new four-note-blues-lick tester. Not much is different here. We assemble four-note licks grouped as eighth-notes in 2/4— half a bar of 4/4, the most common time signature—and we use essentially all of the same production techniques as our sister Three-Note Factory. We offer the same extras, as well: three octaves of licks with multi-tab, "b" phrasing options, "c" melodic variations, handy Applications boxes, and even more optional rhythmic variations.

You know the routine, so punch in and get workin'. As you test each lick in all three octaves—and its greased-up rephrasings and melodic and rhythmic variations—be sure to apply the same rhythmic principles of displacement and melodic permutation you used to expand the three-note licks. (The new group of rhythmic variations at the bottom of each page ensures an inexhaustible supply of fresh four-note licks.) There are 24 (1x2x3x4) melodic permutations for any lick containing four different notes—six starting on each note.

To mix these licks with the previous three-note licks, play them as swung eighth-notes and treat the previous 3/8 groupings as if they were eighth-note triplets. You can also play the four-note licks as straight eighths and convert the 3/8 licks to eighth- and 16th-note groupings. Good luck!

Ex. 1a

A7(I)	2 (3)	R	2	R
D7(IV)	-	-	-	-
E7(V)	5 (6)	4	5	4

1b

1c

A7(I)	2(♭3)	R	2	R
D7(IV)	6(♭7)	5	6	5
E7(V)	5(♭6)	4	5	4

Ex. 2a

A7(I)	R	2	2 (3)	R
D7(IV)	-	-	-	-
E7(V)	4	5	5 (6)	4

2b

*Pre-bend from 4th fret.

2c

A7(I)	R	2	2(♭3)	R
D7(IV)	5	6	6(♭7)	5
E7(V)	4	5	5(♭6)	4

4-note rhythmic variations

Ex. 3a

Applications:				
A7(I)	5	6	R	2 (3)
D7(IV)	-	-	-	-
E7(V)	R	2	4	5(♭6)

Ex. 4a

Applications:				
A7(I)	♭7	R	♭3	4 (5)
D7(IV)	4	5	♭7	R (9)
E7(V)	♭3	4	♭6	♭7(R)

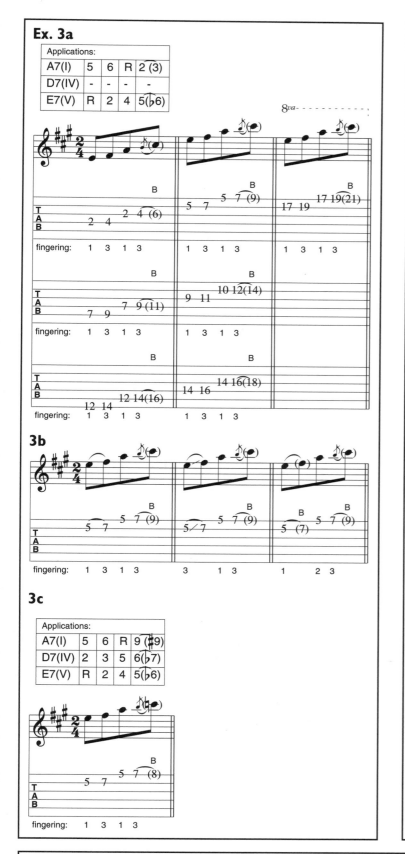

*Pre-bend from 7th fret.

3c

Applications:				
A7(I)	5	6	R	9 (#9)
D7(IV)	2	3	5	6(♭7)
E7(V)	R	2	4	5(♭6)

4c

Applications:				
A7(I)	♭7	R	♭7	4 (5)
D7(IV)	4	5	4	R (9)
E7(V)	♭3	4	#9	♭7R

Ex. 5a

Applications:				
A7(I)	4 (5)	♭3	4	♭3
D7(IV)	R (2)	♭7	R	♭7
E7(V)	♭7(R)	♭6	♭7	♭6

5b

5c

Applications:				
A7(I)	4 (5)	♭3	4	3
D7(IV)	-	-	-	-
E7(V)	♭7(R)	♭6	♭7	6

Applications:				
A7(I)	4(♭5)	♭3	4	♭3
D7(IV)	R(♭9)	♭7	R	♭7
E7(V)	♭7(7)	♭6	♭7	♭6

Ex. 6a

Applications:				
A7(I)	♭3	4	4 (5)	♭3
D7(IV)	♭7	R	R (2)	♭7
E7(V)	♭6	♭7	♭7(R)	♭6

6b

*Pre-bend from 7th fret.

6c

Applications:				
A7(I)	3	4	4 (5)	♭3
D7(IV)	-	-	-	-
E7(V)	6	♭7	♭7(R)	♭6

Applications:				
A7(I)	♭3	4	4 (♭5)	♭3
D7(IV)	♭7	R	R(♭9)	♭7
E7(V)	♭6	♭7	♭7(7)	♭6

Ex. 7a

Applications:				
A7(I)	4 (5)	5	♭5	5
D7(IV)	R (9)	9	♭9	9
E7(V)	♭7(R)	R	7	R

Ex. 8a

Applications:				
A7(I)	♭5	5	♭7	5
D7(IV)	♭9	9	4	9
E7(V)	7	R	♭3	R

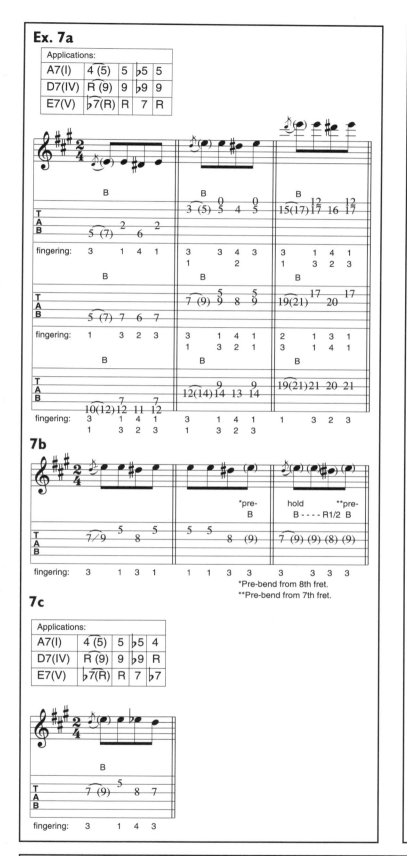

7c

Applications:				
A7(I)	4 (5)	5	♭5	4
D7(IV)	R (9)	9	♭9	R
E7(V)	♭7(R)	R	7	♭7

8c

Applications:				
A7(I)	♭5	5	♭7	♭3
D7(IV)	♭9	9	4	♭7
E7(V)	7	R	♭3	♭6

Applications:				
A7(I)	♭5	5	♭7	3
D7(IV)	-	-	-	-
E7(V)	7	R	♭3	6

Ex. 9a

Applications:				
A7(I)	♭7	5	4	5
D7(IV)	4	2	R	2
E7(V)	♭3	R	♭7	R

9b

9c

Applications:				
A7(I)	♭7	5	4	3
D7(IV)	-	-	-	-
E7(V)	♭3	R	♭7	6

Applications:				
A7(I)	♭7	5	4	♭3
D7(IV)	4	2	R	♭7
E7(V)	♭3	R	♭7	6

Ex. 10a

Applications:				
A7(I)	♭3	R	4	♭3
D7(IV)	♭7	4	R	♭7
E7(V)	♭6	4	♭7	♭6

10b

10c

Applications:				
A7(I)	♭3	R	4	3
D7(IV)	-	-	-	-
E7(V)	♭6	4	♭7	6

Applications:				
A7(I)	3	R	4	♭3
D7(IV)	-	-	-	-
E7(V)	6	4	♭7	♭6

Ex. 13a

Applications:				
A7(I)	4	♭3	R	6
D7(IV)	R	♭7	5	3
E7(V)	♭7	♭6	4	2

Ex. 14a

Applications:				
A7(I)	2(♭3)	2	R	6
D7(IV)	6(♭7)	6	5	3
E7(V)	5(♭6)	5	4	2

13c

Applications:				
A7(I)	♭3	2	R	6
D7(IV)	♭7	6	5	3
E7(V)	♭6	5	4	2

14c

Applications:				
A7(I)	2	(3)	2	R	6
D7(IV)	-	-	-	-
E7(V)	5	(6)	5	4	2

Ex. 15a

Applications:				
A7(I)	4 (5)	4	♭3	R
D7(IV)	R (2)	R	♭7	5
E7(V)	♭7(R)	♭7	6	4

Ex. 16a

Applications:			
A7(I)	4	R	♭3	R
D7(IV)	R	5	♭7	5
E7(V)	♭7	4	♭6	4

15b

16b

**Pre-bend from 7th fret.

15c

Applications:				
A7(I)	4 (5)	4	3	R
D7(IV)	-	-	-	-
E7(V)	♭7(R)	♭7	6	4

16c

Applications:				
A7(I)	R	5	♭7	5
D7(IV)	5	2	4	2
E7(V)	4	R	♭3	R

Applications:				
A7(I)	R	5	♭7	5
D7(IV)	5	2	4	2
E7(V)	4	R	♭3	R

Ex. 17a

Applications:				
A7(I)	R	4 (5)	4	b3
D7(IV)	5	R (2)	R	b7
E7(V)	4	b7(R)	b7	b6

17b

17c

Applications:				
A7(I)	#9	4 (5)	4	b3
D7(IV)	b7	R (2)	R	b7
E7(V)	b6	b7(R)	b7	b6

Ex. 18a

Applications:				
A7(I)	b7(R)	R	b7	5
D7(IV)	4	(5)	5	4	2
E7(V)	b3 (4)	4	b3	R

18b

18c

Applications:				
A7(I)	b7(R)	5	b7	5
D7(IV)	4 (5)	2	4	2
E7(V)	b3 (4)	R	b3	R

Ex. 19a

Applications:				
A7(I)	4 (5)	5	R	♭7
D7(IV)	R (2)	2	5	4
E7(V)	♭7(R)	R	4	♭3

Ex. 20a

Applications:				
A7(I)	4 (5)	5	R	R
D7(IV)	R (2)	2	5	5
E7(V)	♭7(R)	R	4	4

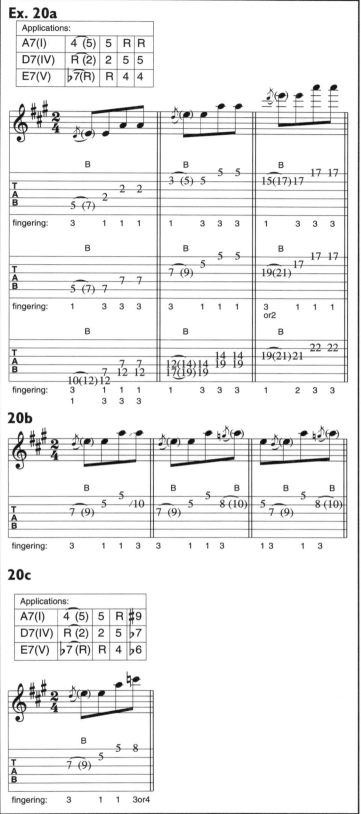

19c

Applications:				
A7(I)	4 (5)	5	R	♭3
D7(IV)	R (2)	2	5	♭7
E7(V)	♭7(R)	R	4	♭6

20c

Applications:				
A7(I)	4 (5)	5	R	♯9
D7(IV)	R (2)	2	5	♭7
E7(V)	♭7(R)	R	4	♭6

Ex. 21a

Applications:				
A7(I)	♭3	3	4	3
D7(IV)	-	-	-	-
E7(V)	♭6	6	♭7	6

Ex. 22a

Applications:				
A7(I)	♭3	3	R	♭7
D7(IV)	-	-	-	-
E7(V)	♭6	6	4	♭3

21c

Applications:				
A7(I)	♭3	3	4	♭3
D7(IV)	♭7	7	R	♭7
E7(V)	♭6	6	♭7	♭6

22c

Applications:				
A7(I)	♭3	3	R	6
D7(IV)	-	-	-	-
E7(V)	♭6	6	4	2

Ex. 23a

Applications:				
A7(I)	♭3	5	♭7	5
D7(IV)	♭7	2	4	2
E7(V)	♭6	R	♭3	R

Ex. 24a

Applications:				
A7(I)	2	R	6	R
D7(IV)	6	5	3	5
E7(V)	5	4	2	4

23c

Applications:				
A7(I)	♭3	5	6	5
D7(IV)	♭7	2	3	2
E7(V)	♭6	R	2	R

24c

Applications:				
A7(I)	♭3	R	6	R
D7(IV)	♭7	5	3	5
E7(V)	♭6	4	2	4

Ex. 25a

Applications:				
A7(I)	/3	5	R	♭7
D7(IV)	-	-	-	-
E7(V)	/6	R	4	♭3

Ex. 26a

Applications:				
A7(I)	/5	♭3	R	5
D7(IV)	/2	♭7	5	2
E7(V)	/R	♭6	4	R

25c

Applications:				
A7(I)	/3	5	R	♯9
D7(IV)	-	-	-	-
E7(V)	/6	R	4	♭6

26c

Applications:				
A7(I)	/5	3	♭7	5
D7(IV)	-	-	-	-
E7(V)	/R	6	♭3	R

CHAPTER 4

FIVE- AND SIX-NOTE BLUES LICKS

Welcome to the Five-Note Blues Lick Factory. Hope those guys down at Four-Note didn't rattle your cage too badly. We run things a little differently around here. The routine is essentially the same as the three- and four-note factories, but with fewer multi-tab fingerings and no Applications boxes. (We use chord symbols to suggest applicable chords.) Here, more of the detailing is left to the end users. We make a progressive product, but we hope that they'll recognize many elements of the licks in Examples 1 through 31 from their past dealings with the company.

We do, however, offer a brand new line of rhythmic variations at the bottom of each page. And, once again, you'll want to apply mileage-enhancing techniques such as rhythmic displacement and melodic permutation—though at 1x2x3x4x5, or 120 combinations, you may just want to concentrate on a handful of favorites.

By the way, since this is a downsized operation, you'll be multi-tasking as a six-note-blues-lick tester during the second half of your shift. Surprise!

Working at the Six-Note Blues Lick Factory may seem cushy at first, but there's a lot more design and engineering expertise involved. The six-note licks in Examples 32 through 51 are our interactive models—they allow users to determine how much finger grease and melodic and rhythmic variation the final product will have. The whole operation has been scaled down to one lick in three octaves with applicable chord symbols. Motivated users can explore multiple fingerings, add or subtract ornaments, and derive melodic and rhythmic variations to create customized six-note licks of their own design. And, of course, they can apply all the previous mileage-enhancing tricks.

Do a good job here, kid, and you'll go far!

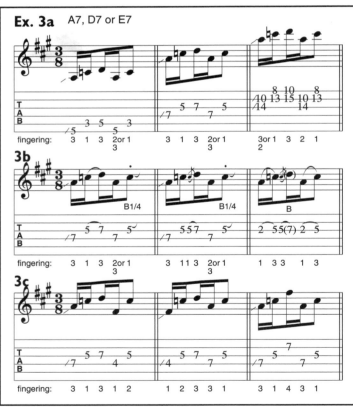

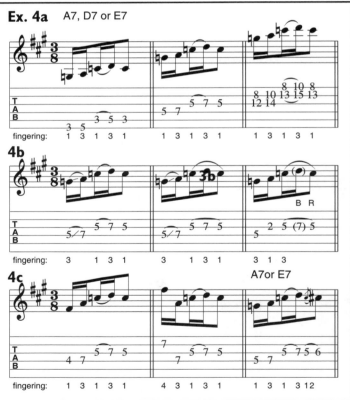

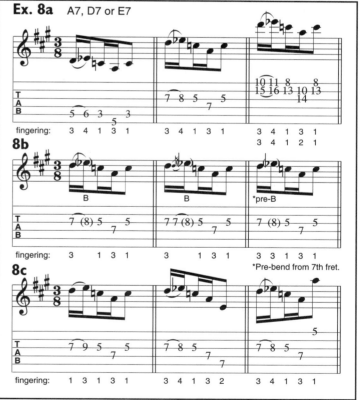

Five- and Six-Note Blues Licks

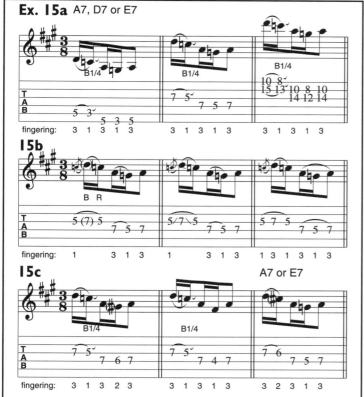

41

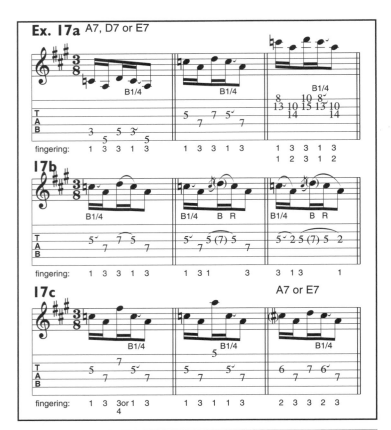

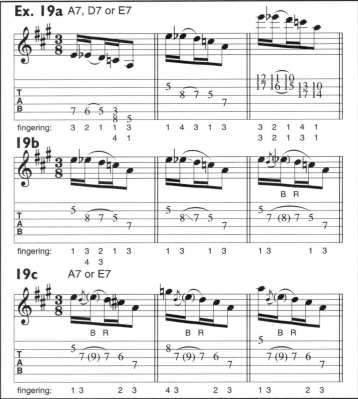

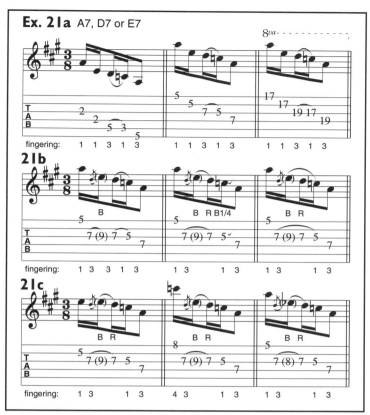

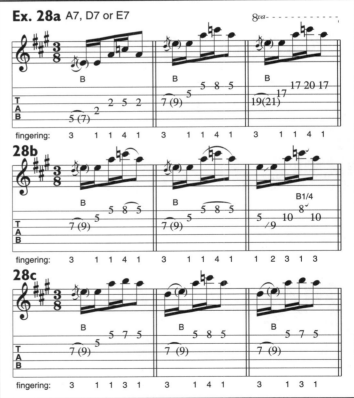

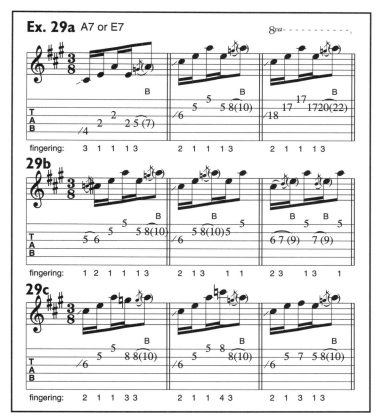

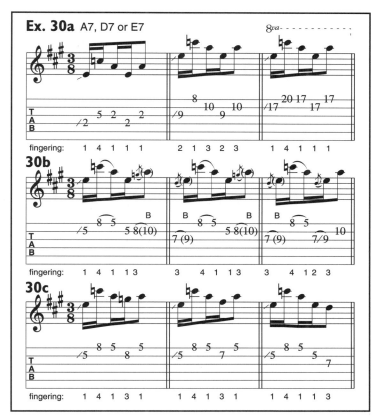

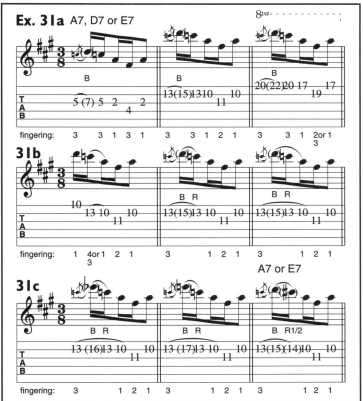

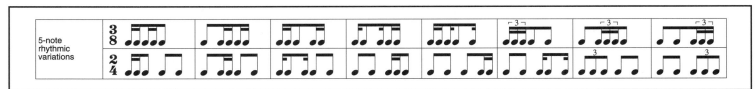

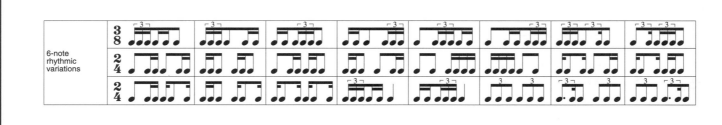

CHAPTER 5

ONE-BAR BLUES LICKS

Welcome to upper management. In addition to making all decisions regarding engineering, production, quality control, and public relations, this is where we determine which three-, four-, five-, and six-note modules match with others to create full bar-long licks.

Your job is to refine Examples 1 through 28—which combine elements of many previous shorter licks—into tasty one-bar statements in both 4/4 and 12/8 feels. This is a prerequisite to your next stage of grooming . . . I mean, development. Perfect these licks and you're headed for CEO territory, my friend. Test them out in all octaves and positions, pepper them with ornaments and melodic/rhythmic variations of your own design, and we'll talk.

Some ground rules: Examples 1–4 illustrate how to convert a 4/4 lick to 12/8, while Examples 5–14 are solid, stand-alone one-bar licks. Finally, Examples 15–24 make use of an eighth-note displacement to create totally new sounds from the same licks. Get it on.

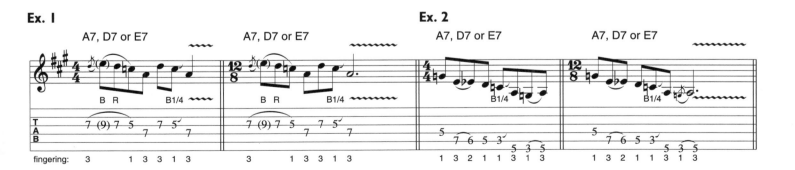

EXTENDED BLUES LINES

Congratulations—you've made it to the top! This is where we design and implement extended lines in the styles of such blues greats as B.B. King, Jimi Hendrix, Mike Bloomfield, Stevie Ray Vaughan, and Robben Ford for use in specific parts of a 12-bar blues progression. You'll recognize many of the moves in these lines from your early days at the three- and four-note facilities, but you'll also discover many new tricks.

We've presented the lines in their order of appearance in both slow- and quick-change 12-bar blues progressions. First, users will expand their rhythmic skills to include converting and adapting 12/8 rhythms to 4/4. Ex. 1 shows how to convert a 12/8 lick (bar 1) into 4/4 (bar 2) before adapting it to an eighth- and 16th-note–based 4/4 motif (bar 3). Examples 2, 3, and 4 follow suit, minus the 4/4 conversion.

Ex. 1

Ex. 2

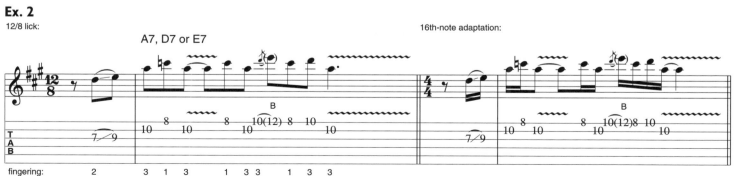

Ex. 3

12/8 lick: 16th-note adaptation:

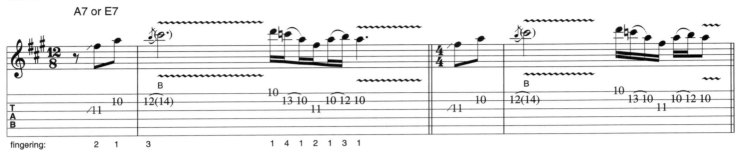

Ex. 4

12/8 lick: 16th-note adaptation:

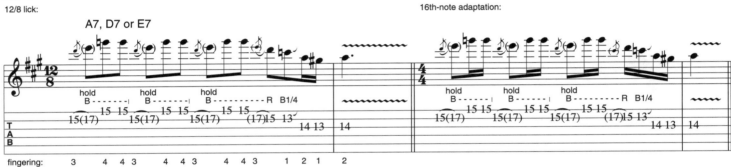

Examples 5–16 are pickup lines designed to approach the downbeat of bar 1.

Ex. 5

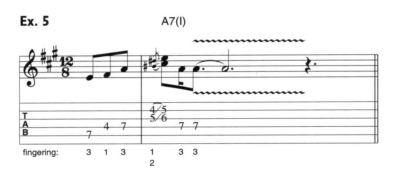

Ex. 6

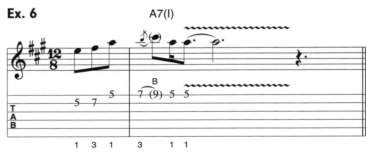

Ex. 7

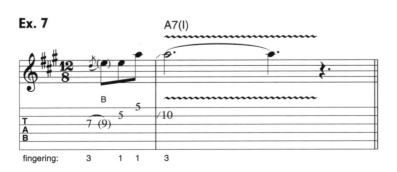

Ex. 8

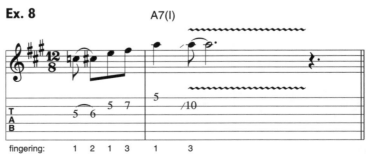

Ex. 9

Ex. 10

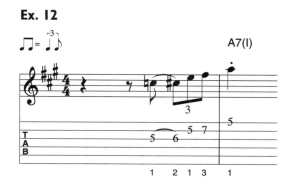

Ex. 11

Ex. 12

Ex. 13

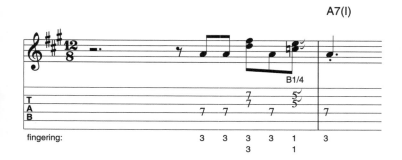

Ex. 14

Ex. 15

Ex. 16

Examples 17 and 18 show two complete four-bar intro figures. Ex. 17 comprises standard single-note licks, while Ex. 18 maps out a mix of reversed *A7* and *Ab7* arpeggios with a single-note follow-up.

Ex. 17

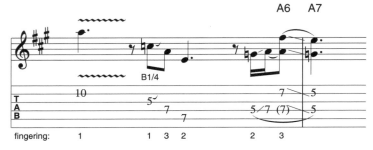

Ex. 18

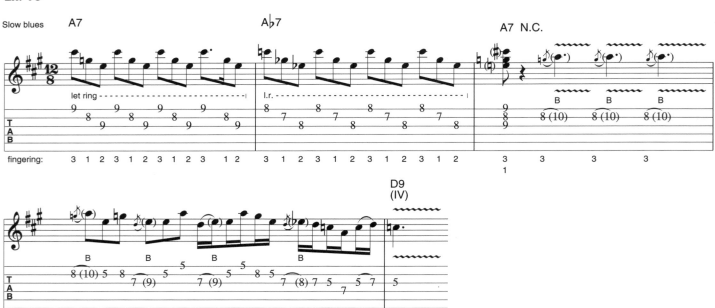

Examples 19–22 are I-chord lines, suitable for dropping into bars 1–4, 7, 8, 11, and 12 of a slow-change blues, or bars 1, 2, 4, 7, 8, and 11 of a quick-change progression. Examples 19 and 20 are one-bar lines, while Examples 21 and 22 span two bars each. (Hint: Any *A* blues I-chord line without a *C#* will work equally well for the IV and V chords.)

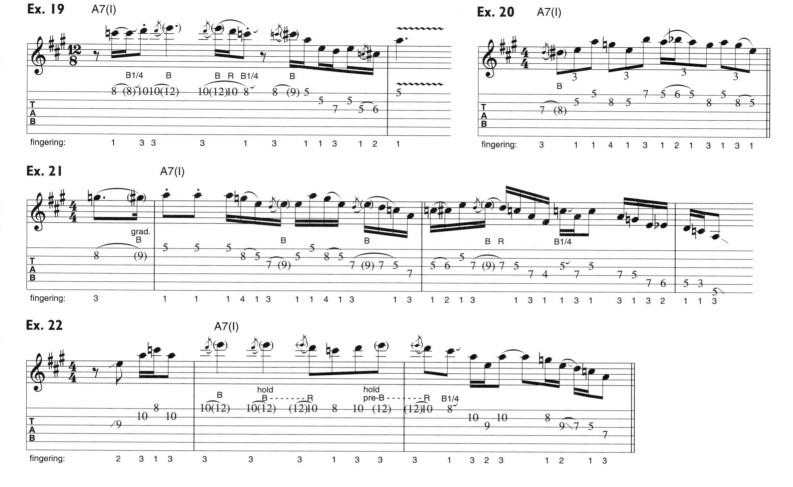

Examples 23 and 24 navigate the I–IV change found in bars 4 and 5 of a slow-change progression as well as in bars 1 and 2 of a quick-change blues.

Ex. 23

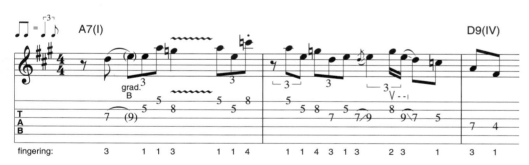

Ex. 24

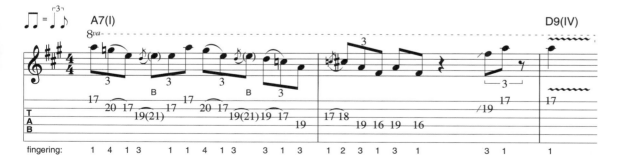

Examples 25 and 26 nail the move from IV back to I—bars 5 and 6 into bar 7 of a slow change, plus bar 2 to 3 in a quick change.

Ex. 25

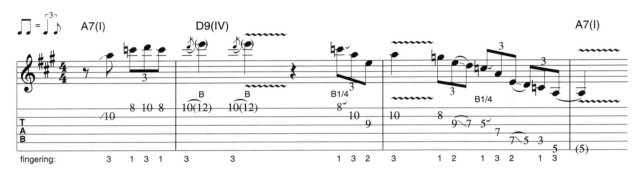

Ex. 26

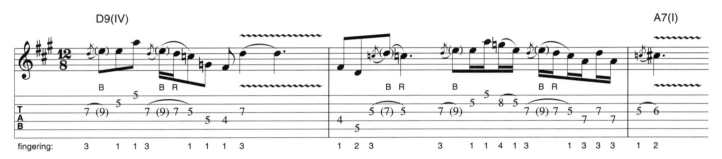

The lines in Examples 27 and 28 originated over the I–V change (bars 7 and 8 into bar 9), but could easily be dropped into any part of a 12-bar progression, slow or quick change.

Ex. 27

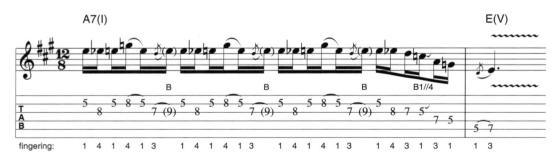

Ex. 28

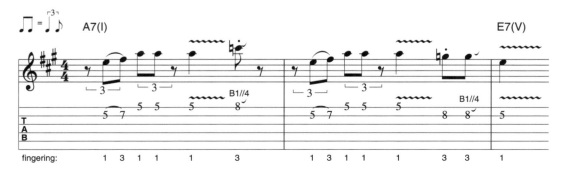

We'll call it a day with the four turnarounds in Examples 29–32: two in 4/4 and two in 12/8. The turnaround (bars 11 and 12) is the blues guitarist's watering hole—a place to visit for rejuvenation at the end of each 12-bar chorus's toils. Pet turnarounds abound; as I've often noted, you can tell a lot about a player by his turnarounds.

Ex. 29

Ex. 30

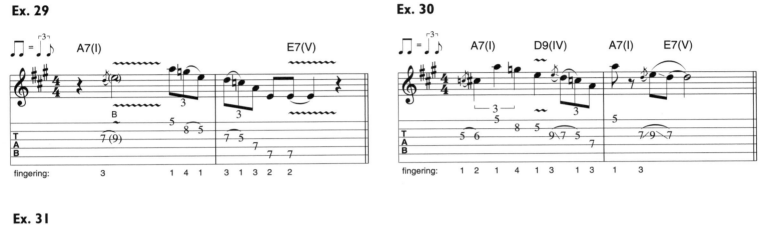

Ex. 31

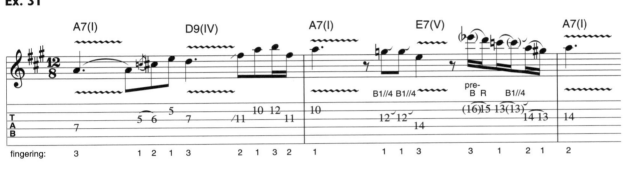

Ex. 32

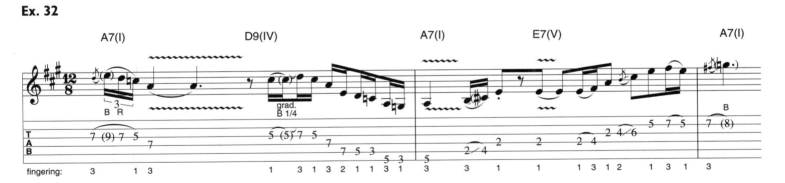

As our ace beta tester, you should now be equipped with enough licks and lines to jam the blues all night. Bravo—you've done a fine job . . . I'm sorry, what was your name again? Well, there's a big bonus for you, and you'll have a week off to enjoy the fruits of your labors, but guess what? You've done all you can do here, so you're being transferred to the Rock Lick Factory. But don't worry—you're still in the family!

CHAPTER 7

ROCK LICK FACTORY TOUR

Welcome to the Rock Lick Factory. Glad to have you aboard. Your job in this facility is a contract deal—no raises or promotions; just a pile of steady work. We have a different marketing strategy and approach to production than our sister blues factory. Because of its inexorable historical connection to pop culture for more than four decades, rock 'n' roll has evolved considerably more than blues, even though licks in both genres are constructed from the same raw materials using similar techniques. The licks we manufacture here are designed to reflect an awareness of this connection and chronology.

You'll begin by refining some of the earliest rock 'n' roll licks, first assembled by such pioneers as Scotty Moore, Carl Perkins, James Burton, Cliff Gallup, and Chuck Berry in the late '50s and early '60s. Next, you'll test-drive our line of late-'60s/early-'70s licks, modeled after the heroes of the British blues-rock boom (Eric Clapton, Jeff Beck, and Jimmy Page) and their U.S. allies (Jimi Hendrix, Johnny Winter, Todd Rundgren, Steve Miller, and Joe Walsh). Finally, you'll finish your tenure in our contemporary rock division, which reflects the super-chops movement spearheaded by '80s innovators Edward Van Halen, Steve Vai, and Joe Satriani.

This is where your previous experience at the Blues Lick Factory pays off. Rock guitarists have been hot-rodding the blues and mining the genre for decades. You'll find that all of the scales and techniques used in blues resurface in rock music. However, once we exit the '70s, you'll need to understand major and minor scales in order to get the most out of our contemporary rock licks.

Here are the *A* major and *A* minor scales, written out in their entirety as well as broken into five distinct fretboard patterns. Look closely and you'll find that these scales are identical to the major pentatonic and minor pentatonic scales (see page 2), but with two extra notes each. For the major scale, degrees 4 and 7 (*D* and *G♯* in the key of *A*) are added to the major pentatonic scale. To form the minor scale, degrees 2 and ♭6 (*B* and *F♮* in *A* minor) are inserted into the minor pentatonic scale. We recommend you memorize these major- and minor-scale patterns, and then transpose them to all keys.

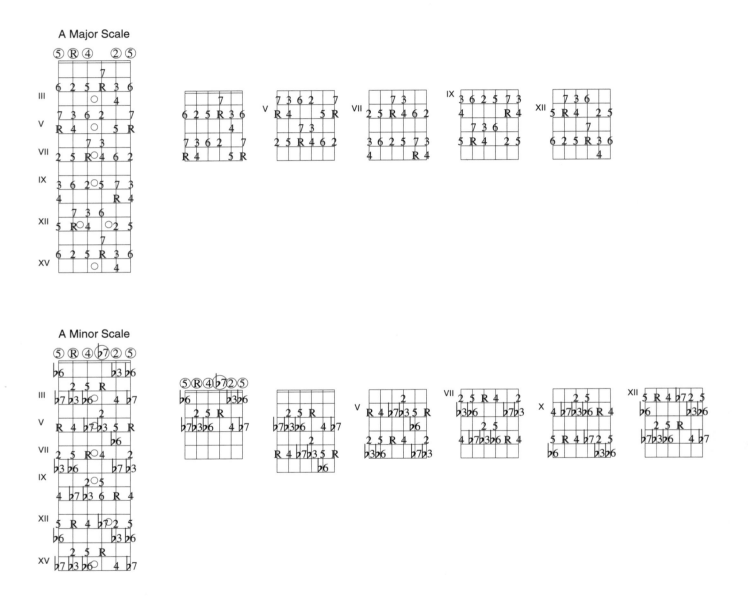

Though we don't supply the abundance of accoutrements that you enjoyed in the blues factory, those extras, along with mileage enhancers like rhythmic displacement and melodic permutation, are ideally suited and highly recommended for use in the Rock Lick Factory. That wraps up the tour—it's time to get to work!

EARLY ROCK 'N' ROLL LICKS

Our early rock 'n' roll licks are ideal for using in souped-up rockabilly-style 12-bar blues progressions. We've presented each lick in a single octave and tab position, and we've included one or more chord symbols that indicate its application to the I (*A7*), IV (*D7*), and V (*E7*) chords.

Each of the first 88 licks spans a full measure of 4/4, while the last dozen are two-bar licks. All fall into three categories: single-note licks, double-stop licks, or licks that combine both. Notice that unlike the blues, many of these early rock 'n' roll moves feature more sliding than bending. (Understandable, since the guys playing them were still using heavy-gauge strings with wound *G*'s!)

Many of our customers have had great success mixing and matching one-bar "modules" over jumping rockabilly progressions. We highly recommend pairing the following one-bar licks into two-bar phrases. Try Examples 13 and 14, Examples 72 and 79, Examples 63 and 73, Examples 83 and 47, Examples 78 and 82, Examples 16 and 33, and Examples 58 and 55. Once you get the hang of these, you can tack on additional licks to form even longer phrases.

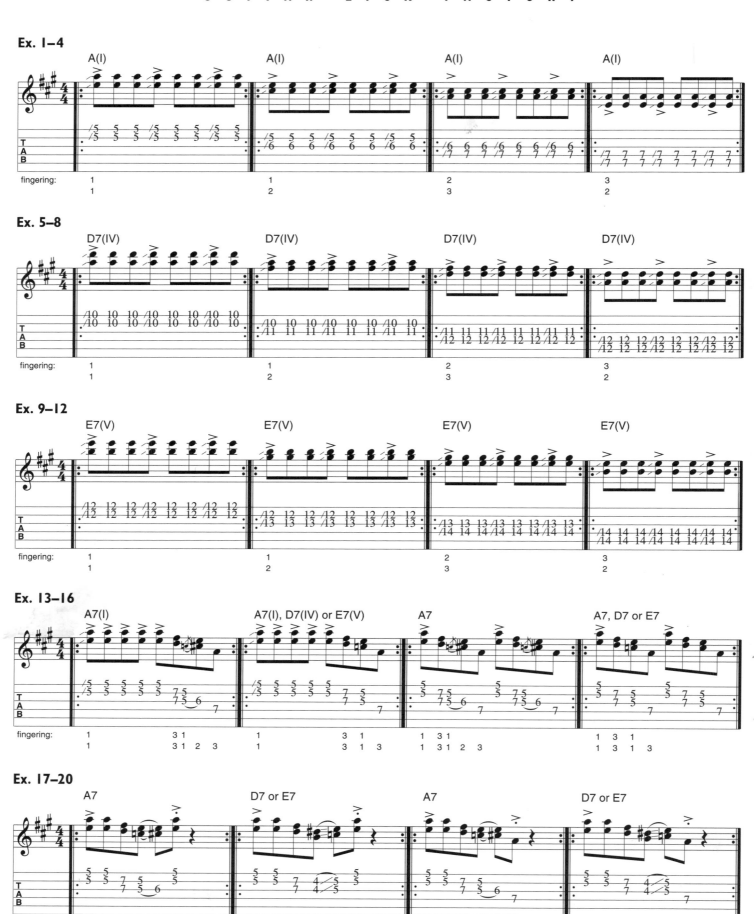

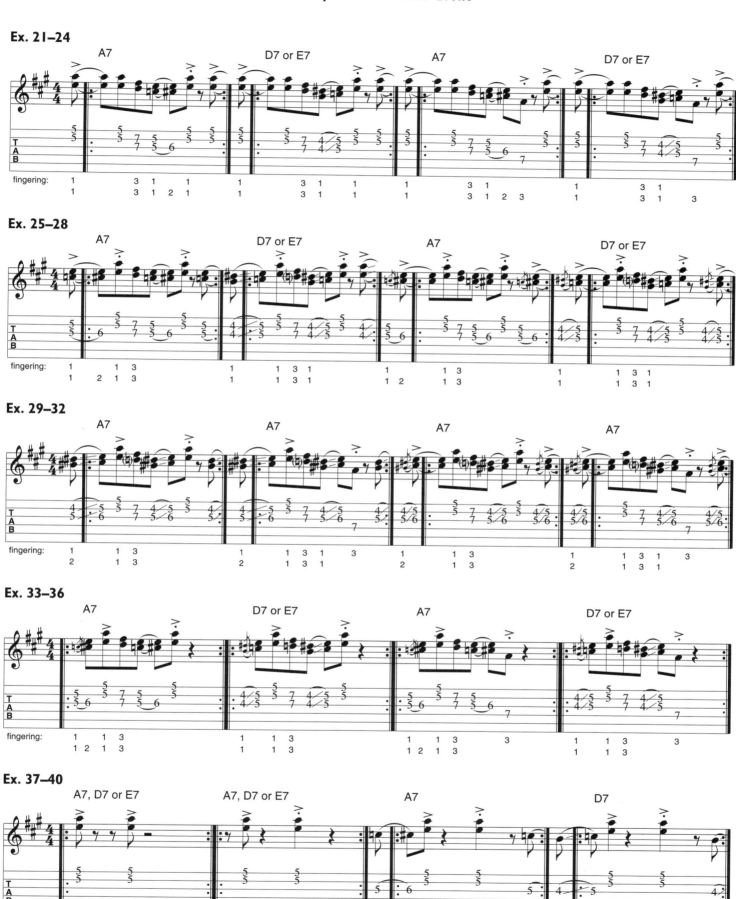

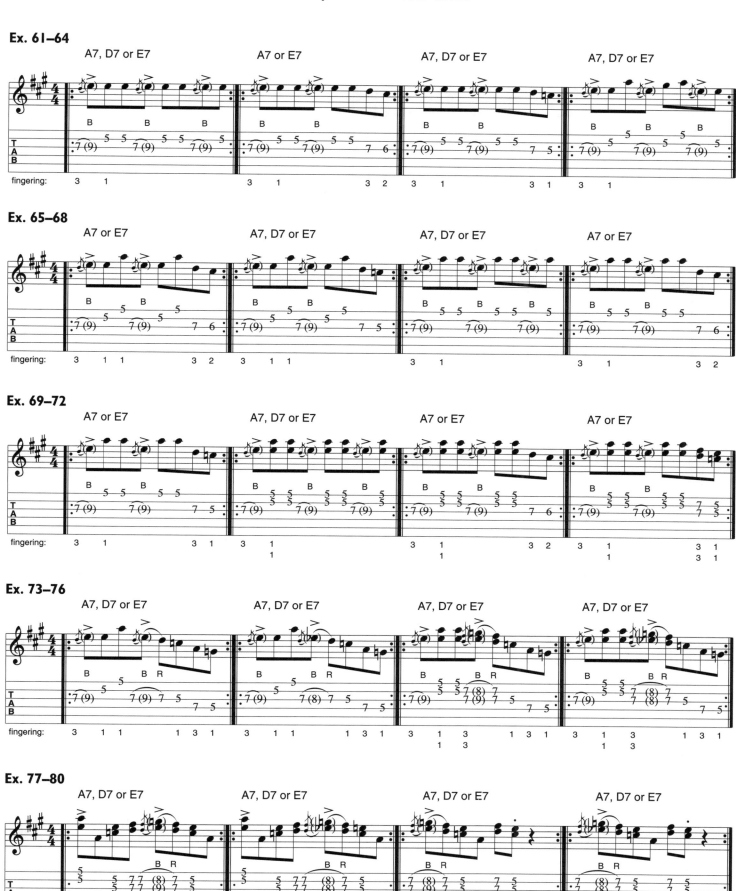

Ex. 81–84

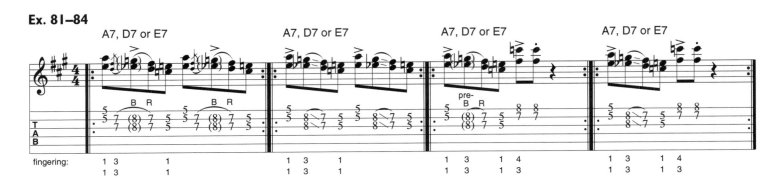

Ex. 85–88

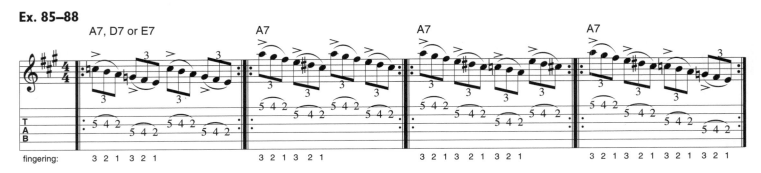

Ex. 89–90

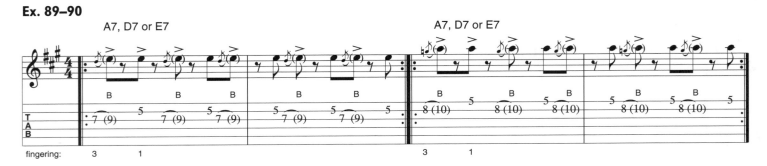

Ex. 91–92

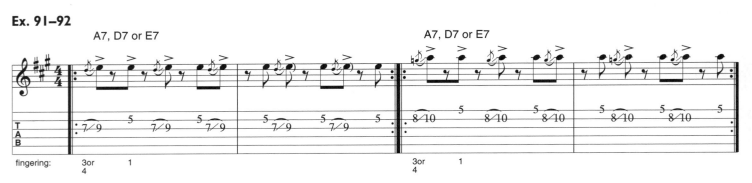

Ex. 93–94

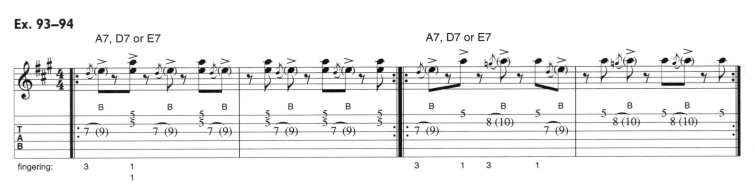

Ex. 95–96

Ex. 97–98

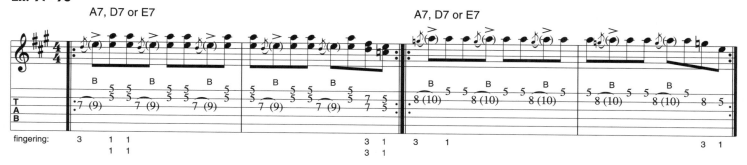

Ex. 99–100

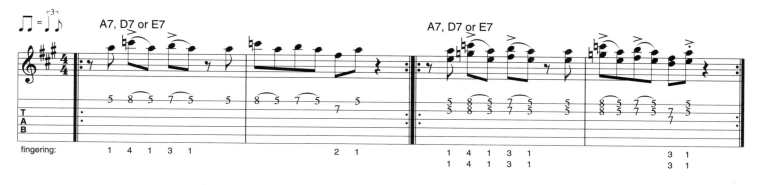

CHAPTER 9

ONE-BAR '60s AND '70s ROCK LICKS

You'll find numerous ties between our early rock 'n' roll and '60s/'70s rock departments. In fact, many of our '60s/'70s models are rewired, hopped-up, or bent-up versions of early rock 'n' roll licks. For instance, Examples 1–3 show how to induce additional motion from early rock 'n' roll double-stops. By now, you should be very familiar with this "3–3–2" eighth-note grouping.

A key component in this evolution was the advent of extra-light-gauge strings, which included an unwound *G* and facilitated easier and more accurate string bends. Maintaining the same previous rhythmic motif, the next three licks (Examples 4–6) reiterate a trio of Old School moves in preparation for the wild bending action in Examples 7–59. Be sure to repeat all examples at least four times.

While the majority of these licks work equally well in beefed-up 12-bar progressions—a staple of '60s and '70s rockers—we chose to show their application over four different chord types built from an *A* root: *A*, *A7*, *Am7*, and *A7#9*. Most of the *A*, *A7*, and *A7#9* licks are interchangeable, and some also work for *Am7*. (Hint: *Am7* licks sound great with *D9*, the IV chord in the key of *A*.) Of course, you'll want to transpose them to all keys.

Every lick in Examples 1–59 features eight consecutive eighth-notes. Examples 36a–36h illustrate how to derive eight displaced variations from a single one-bar lick. Ex. 36a shows a given lick. Ex. 36b displaces this lick by moving its second note back to beat *one*, while the first note jumps to the end of the measure. Ex. 36c starts on the third note of the original lick, Ex. 36d starts on the fourth note, and so on. Since this occurs within a single measure, you could also view it as "rhythmic permutation" or "melodic displacement." Using this method, you can create eight customized versions of each one-bar lick.

Ex. 1–3

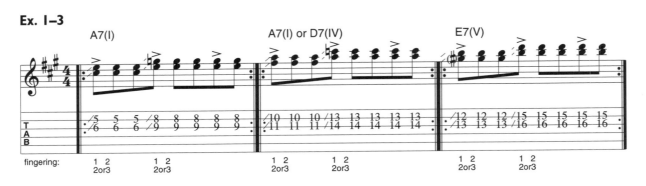

Ex. 4–7

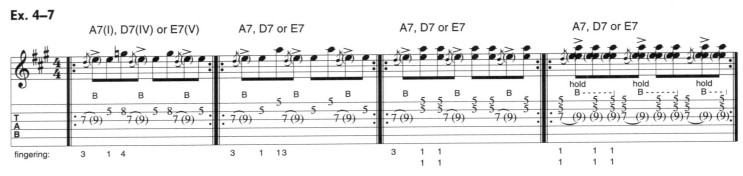

Ex. 8–11

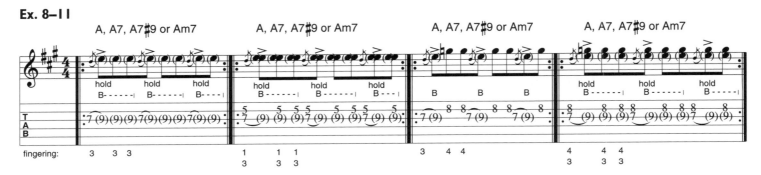

Ex. 12–15

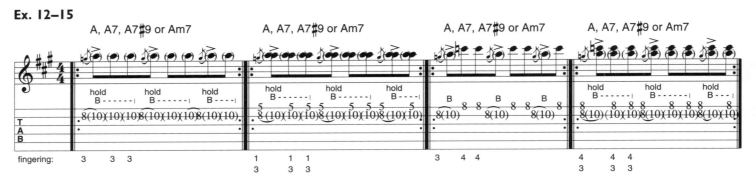

Ex. 16–19

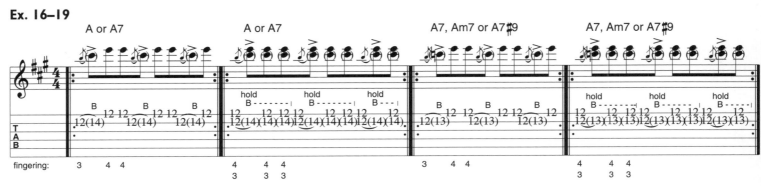

One-Bar '60s and '70s Rock Licks

Ex. 20–23

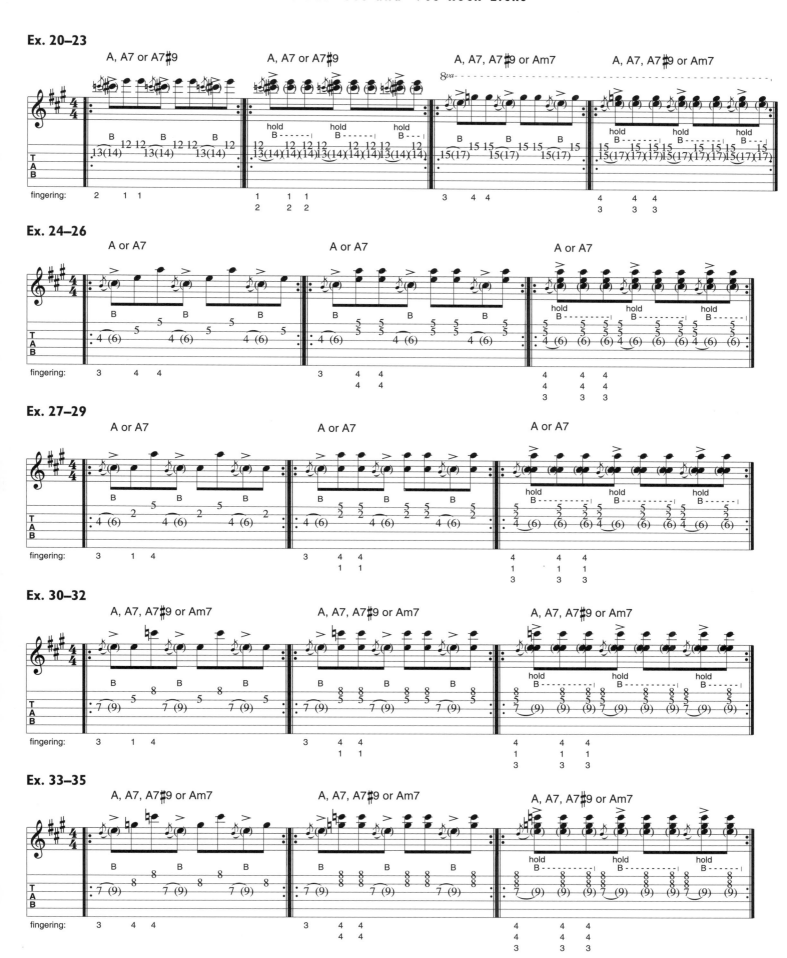

Ex. 24–26

Ex. 27–29

Ex. 30–32

Ex. 33–35

Ex. 36a, b, c, d

Given: A, A7, Am7, or A7#9

fingering: 3   1   1   1   1   3   1   3   1   3   1   1

Ex. 36e, f, g, h

fingering: 1   1   3   1   3   1   3   1   1   1   3   1

Ex. 37–40

A, A7, A7#9 or Am7   A, A7, A7#9 or Am7   A, A7, A7#9 or Am7   A or A7

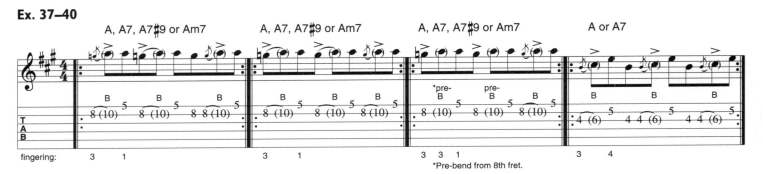

 fingering: 3   1   3   1   3   3   1   3   4

*Pre-bend from 8th fret.

Ex. 41–44

A or A7   A or A7   A or A7   A or A7

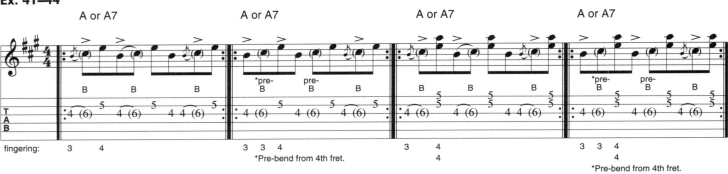

 fingering: 3   4   3   3   4   3   4   3   3   4
                                  *Pre-bend from 4th fret.   4   4

*Pre-bend from 4th fret.

Ex. 45–48

A, A7, A7#9 or Am7   A, A7, A7#9 or Am7   A, A7, A7#9 or Am7

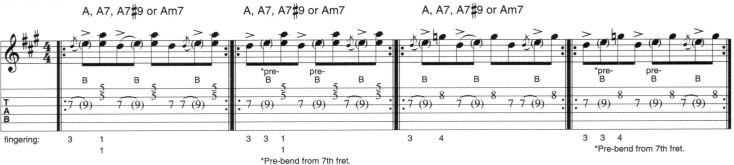

fingering: 3   1   3   3   1   3   4   3   3   4
            1   1
                  *Pre-bend from 7th fret.   *Pre-bend from 7th fret.

One-Bar '60s and '70s Rock Licks

Ex. 49–52

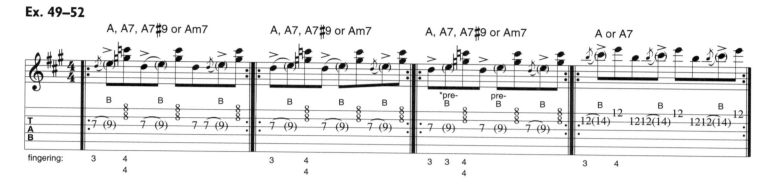

Ex. 53–56

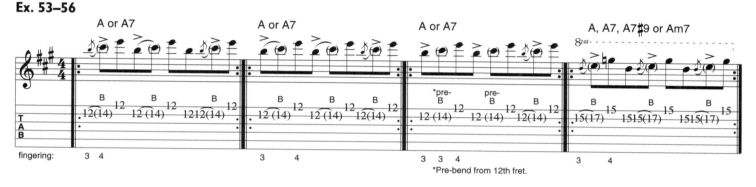

*Pre-bend from 12th fret.

Ex. 57–59

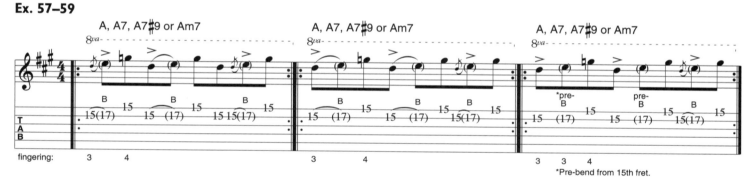

*Pre-bend from 15th fret.

CHAPTER 10

'60s AND '70s POWER-TRIO LICKS

When power trios became the rage during the '60s and '70s, rock guitarists found themselves with a lot of space to fill. One logical response was to lay down sheets of repetitive 16th-note–based licks. The Rock Lick Factory manufactures an impressive line of '60s and '70s power-trio licks (Examples 1–49). Each comes complete and ready to repeat with notated chord applications. Get to know them.

We also offer 20 custom rhythmic and phrasing variations for each lick (Examples 50–69).

Ex. 1–4

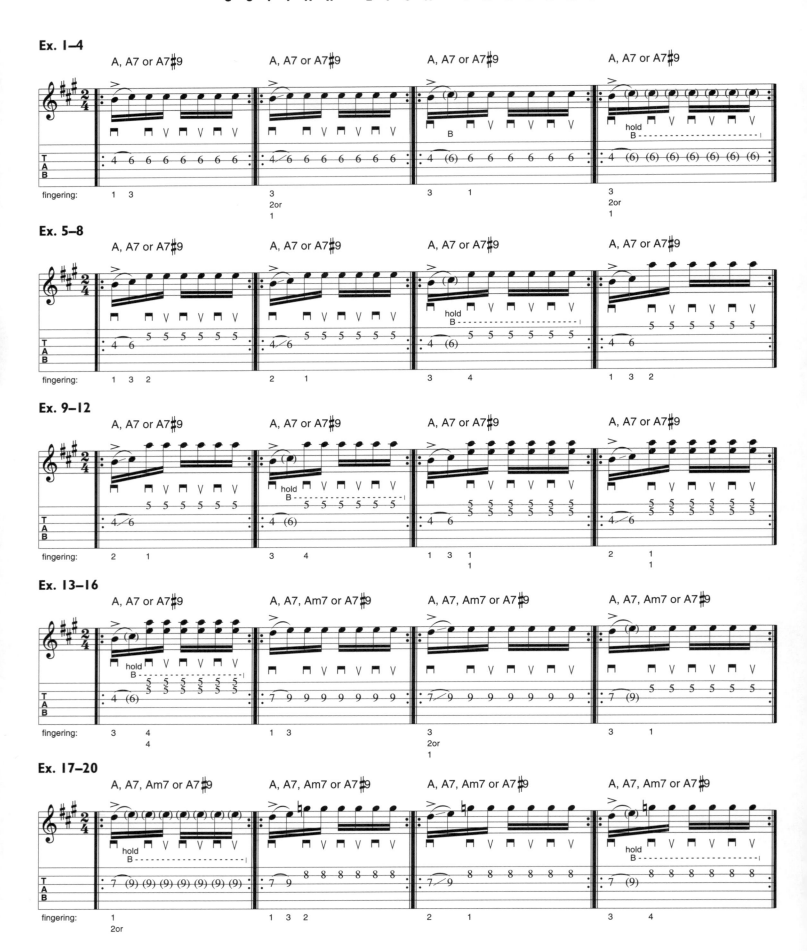

Ex. 5–8

Ex. 9–12

Ex. 13–16

Ex. 17–20

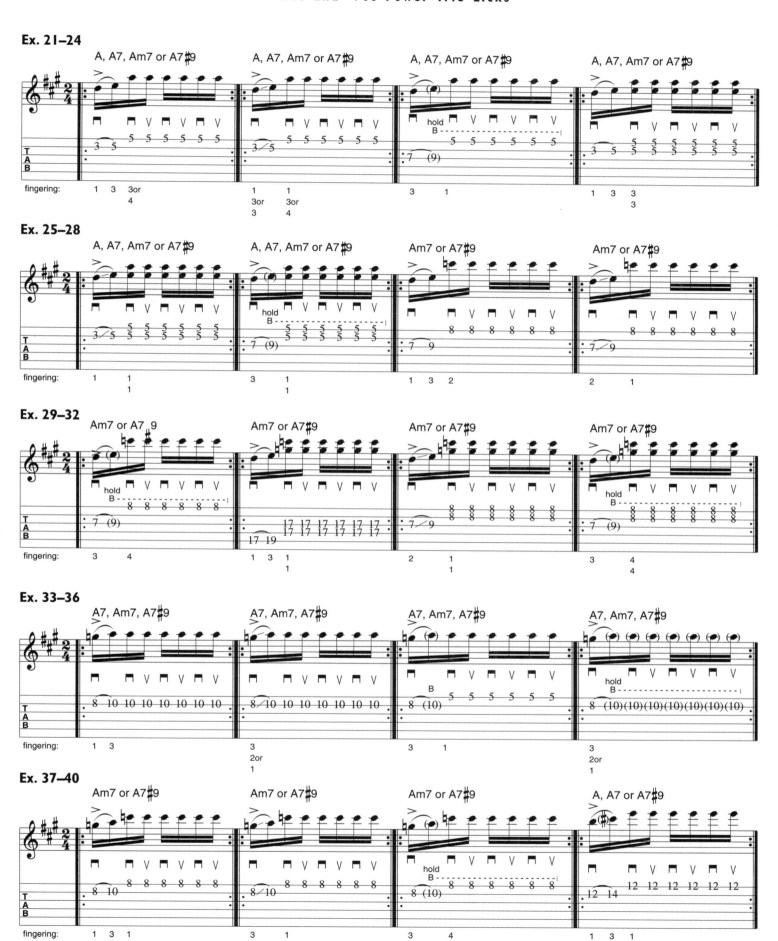

Ex. 61–63

A, A7, A7#9 or Am7

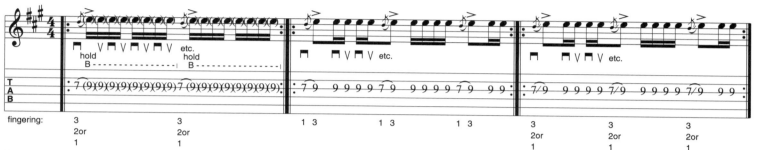

Ex. 64–66

A, A7, A7#9 or Am7

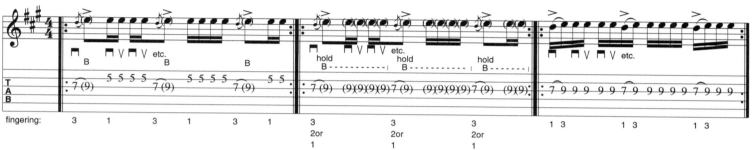

Ex. 67–69

A, A7, A7#9 or Am7

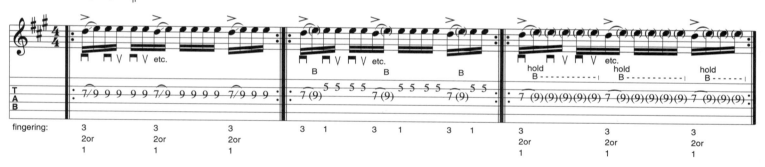

CHAPTER 11

PENTATONIC SEQUENCES AND SPEED LICKS

Pentatonic scale sequences play a huge role in the '60s/'70s rock guitar vocabulary. Sequencing a scale involves arranging its notes into equal groupings in some sort of numerical order. The grouping is then repeated starting on each scale step: 1–2–3, 2–3–4, 3–4–5, 4–5–6, etc. Translated to *A* pentatonic minor, this would be played root–♭3–4, ♭3–4–5, 4–5–♭7, 5–♭7–root (*A–C–D, C–D–E, D–E–G, E–G–A*), etc. Get the idea?

Examples 1–10 illustrate a variety of sequences derived from three-, four-, and five-note groupings of the *A* pentatonic minor and *A* pentatonic major scales. Try to spot the numerical sequences in each one, and then create a few of your own.

The 14 one-bar "speed licks" that follow (Examples 11–24) were built by taking sections of these and similar *A* pentatonic minor, *A* pentatonic major, and *A* blues scale sequences and fragmenting them into short, repetitive motifs. They all come with three-octave notation and multi-tab as standard features. Notice how you pick only four times per measure; all of the other notes are hammer-ons or pull-offs. Pay close attention to the pick-hand notation, especially the two consecutive downstrokes you use to play the last 16th-note of beat *one* and the first 16th-note of beat *two*. Use a continuous, uninterrupted downstroke to create a smooth flow between these two notes on adjacent strings. In Examples 11–18, the same action occurs between the last and first notes of the measure each time you repeat the lick. In Examples 19–24, the opening note is picked the first time it is played, and then hammered-on for each repeat.

Ex. 1

A Pentatonic Minor sequences:

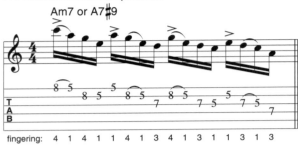

Ex. 2

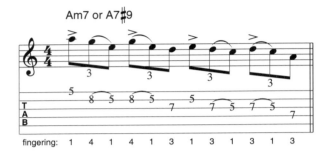

Ex. 3

Ex. 4

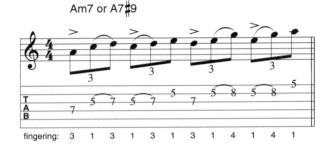

Ex. 5

A Pentatonic Major sequences:

Ex. 6

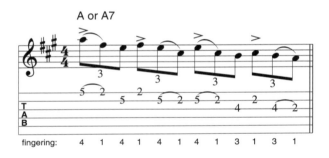

Ex. 7

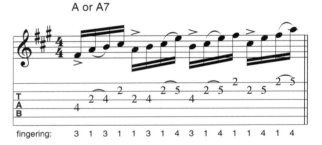

Ex. 8

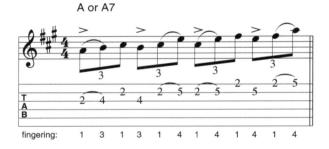

Ex. 9

Five-note A Pentatonic Minor sequences:

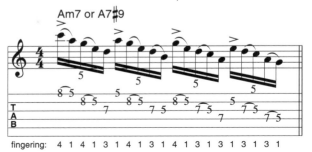

Ex. 10

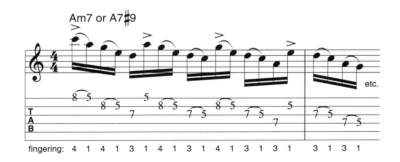

Ex. 11   A Pentatonic Minor or A Blues

Ex. 12   A Blues

Ex. 13   A Pentatonic Minor or A Blues

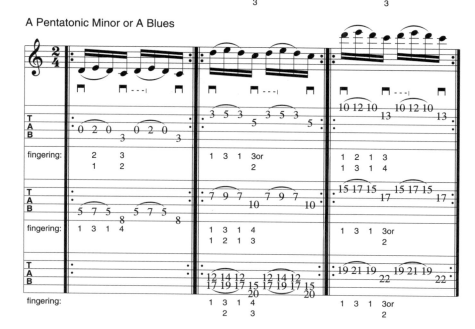

Ex. 14   A Blues

Ex. 15   A Pentatonic Minor or A Blues

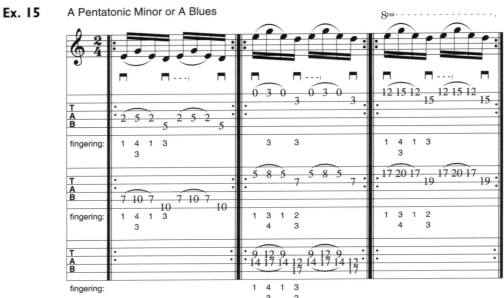

Ex. 16   A Blues

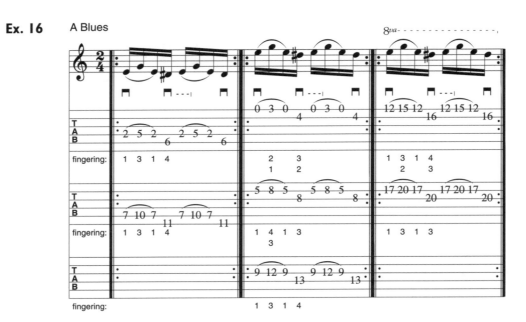

Pentatonic Sequences and Speed Licks

Ex. 17   A Pentatonic Minor or A Blues

Ex. 18   A Pentatonic Minor or A Blues

Ex. 19   A Blues

Ex. 20   A Pentatonic Minor or A Blues

Ex. 21   A Pentatonic Major

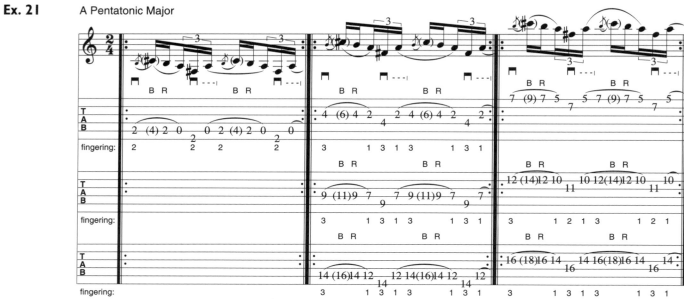

Ex. 22   A Pentatonic Major/Minor combination

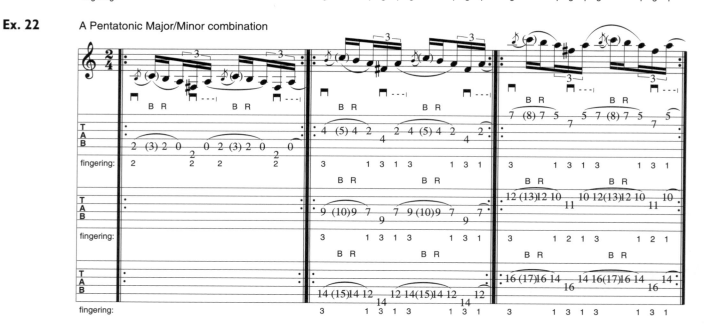

Ex. 23

A Pentatonic Minor or A Blues

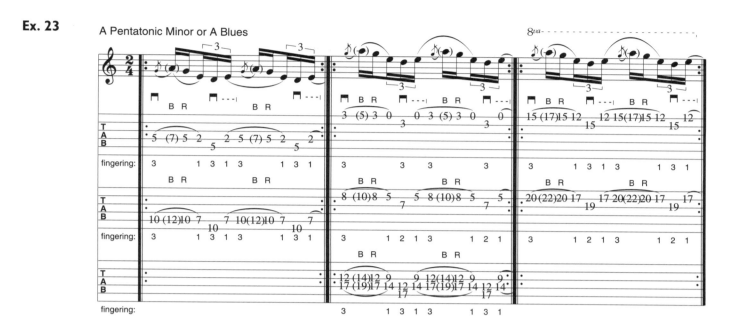

Ex. 24

A Blues

CHAPTER 12

FOUR-NOTE CONTEMPORARY ROCK LICKS AND MODAL SEQUENCES

As we mentioned during your tour, our Contemporary Rock Division takes full advantage of the extra notes offered by the major and minor scales to produce an impressive line of licks, including major, minor, and modal sequences. These additional scale tones encourage a more scalar/modal approach to licks and melodies, a trend that began developing back in the late '70s—possibly in reaction to the guitar-repressive disco era that preceded it.

Ex. 1 suggests a dozen phrasing options for the three-octave multi-tabbed licks in Examples 2–17. You can play the four-note *A* major licks in Examples 2–9 over any diatonic triad or 7th chord in the key of *A*: *A, Bm, C#m, D, E, F#m,* and *G#dim,* or *Amaj7, Bm7, C#m7, Dmaj7, E7, F#m7,* and *G#m7b5.* The four-note *A* minor licks in Examples 10–17 work equally well with any diatonic triad or 7th chord in *A* minor: *Am, Bdim, C, Dm, Em, F,* and *G,* or *Am7, Bm7b5, Cmaj7, Dm7, Em7, Fmaj7,* and *G7* (See *The Guitar Cookbook* to discover how these chords are formed in all keys). Again, you may have to add a target tone to fit the chord of the moment. Each of these four-note licks is designed to stand on its own, but if you choose an octave and follow it through the *A* major licks in Examples 2–9, you'll hear an *A* major scale sequence emerge. Similarly, you can use the same method to derive an *A* minor scale sequence from the four-note *A* minor licks in Examples 10–17. Remember to transpose these licks and sequences to all keys.

Examples 18–21 adapt these licks to four parallel modal sequences: *A* Lydian, *A* Mixolydian, *A* Dorian, and *A* Phrygian. Each one is notated in a single octave (with suggested chord symbols) and played on the same string. To form *A* Lydian, we simply raise the 4 (*D*) of the *A* major scale (also known as *A* Ionian) one half-step to make it the #4 (*D#*). For *A* Mixolydian, we lower the 7 (*G#*) of the *A* major scale one half-step to the ♭7 (*G*). *A* Dorian and *A* Phrygian are both derived from the *A* minor scale (also known as *A* Aeolian). For *A* Dorian, we raise the ♭6 (*F*) one half-step to the 6 (*F#*), and for *A* Phrygian we lower the 2 (*B*) one half-step to the ♭2 (*B♭*). Ex. 22 shows seven phrasing options for Examples 23–26, which sequentially navigate a new lick through the same four modes. You can play all of these modal sequences in reverse or descending order.

Ex. 27 shows how to create an ascending *A* Dorian sequence using a pick/bend/release/pull-off move in each measure, while the *A* Mixolydian sequence in Ex. 28 hints at the potential advantages of spreading these licks across adjacent strings. Be sure to play both sequences in ascending and descending order.

Ex. 1

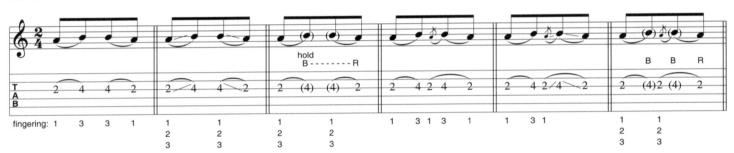

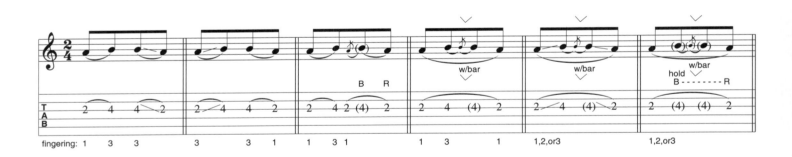

Four-Note Contemporary Rock Licks and Modal Sequences

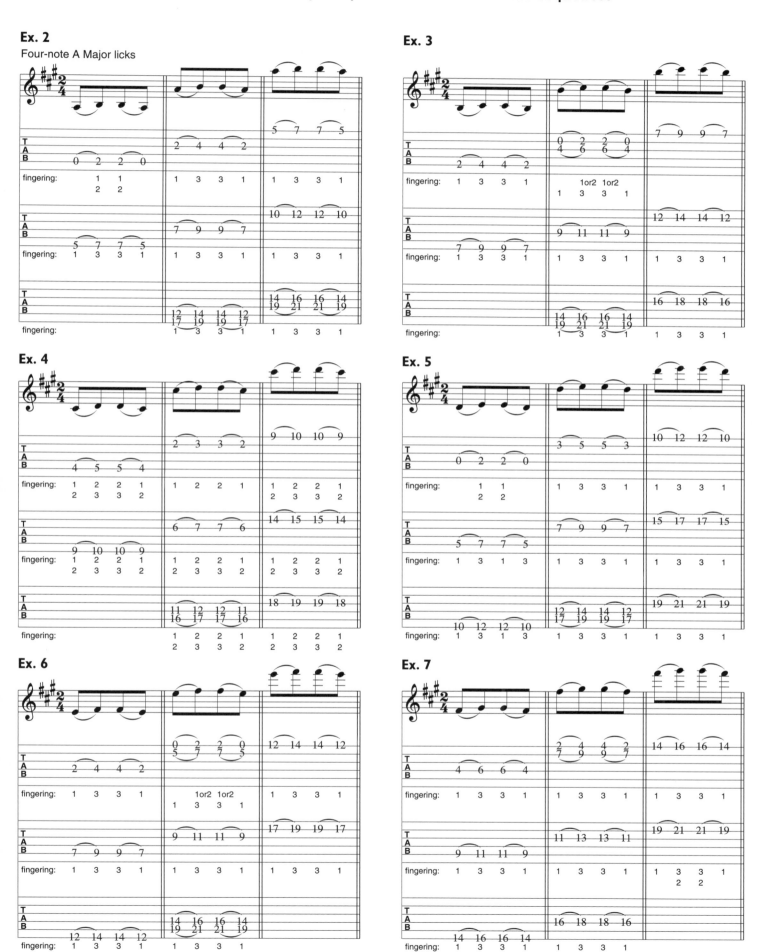

Ex. 8

Ex. 9

Ex. 10

Four-note A Minor licks

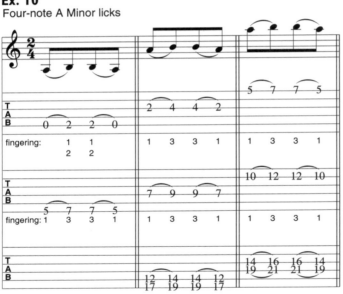

Ex. 11

Ex. 12

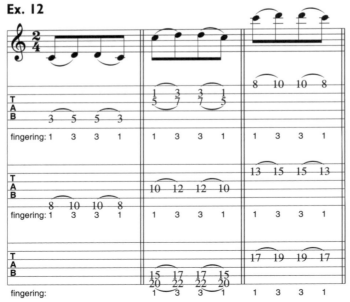

Ex. 13

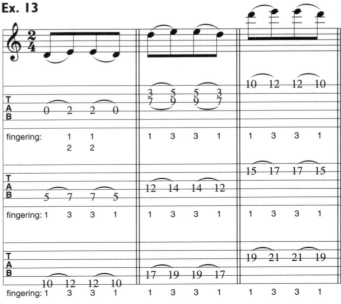

Ex. 14

Ex. 15

Ex. 16

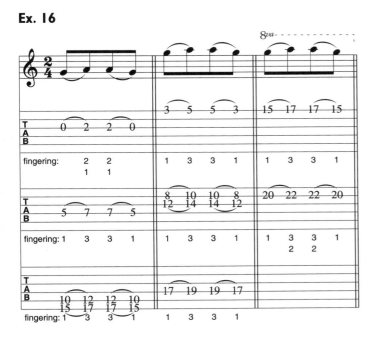

Ex. 17

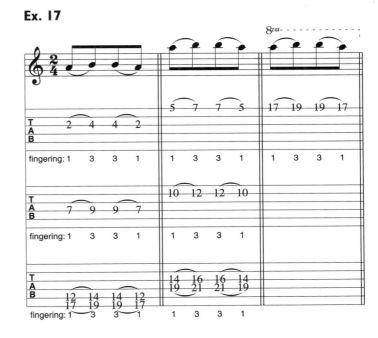

Ex. 18

A Lydian

A or Amaj7(♯11)

Ex. 19

A Mixolydian

Ex. 20

A Dorian

Ex. 21

A Phrygian

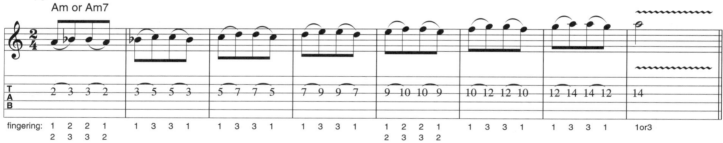

Ex. 22

Phrasing variations for next four examples:

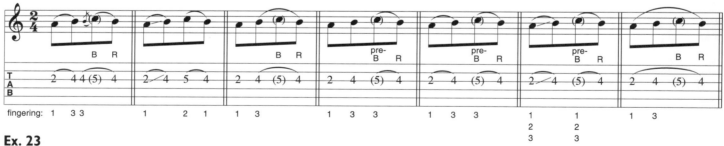

Ex. 23

A Dorian

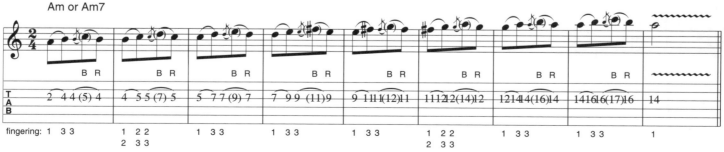

Ex. 24

A Mixolydian

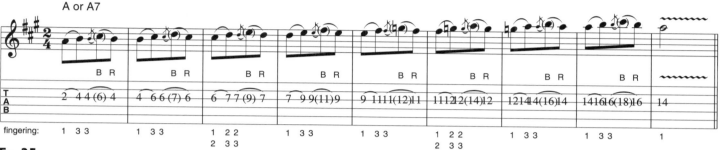

Ex. 25

A Lydian

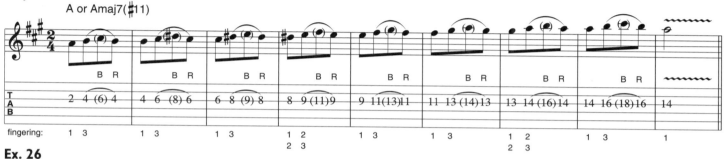

Ex. 26

A Phrygian

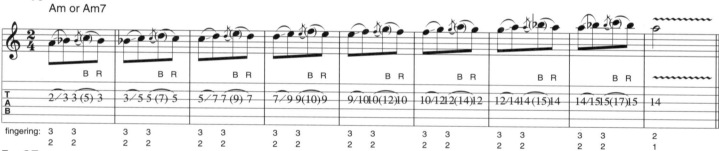

Ex. 27

A Dorian

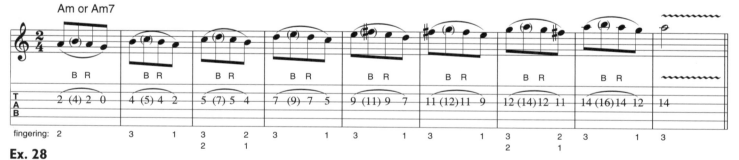

Ex. 28

A Mixolydian

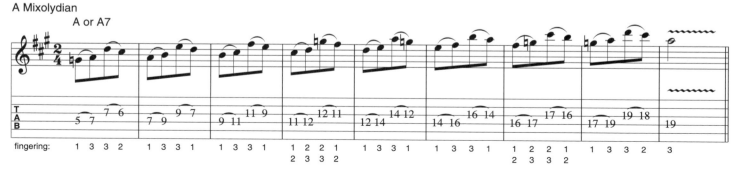

CHAPTER 13

CONTEMPORARY ROCK SPEED LICKS

The contemporary rock speed licks in Examples 1–8 follow the same format as our '60s/'70s speed licks. We've notated all in three octaves with multi-tab, but in *A Dorian* only. Again, these are designed as stand-alone licks, but you can form a speedy *A Dorian* sequence by playing each lick in Examples 1–8 in rapid succession within a single octave. And yes, it sounds as good descending as it does ascending. These licks also work well over all diatonic triads and 7th chords of *A Dorian*: *Am, Bm, C, D, Em, F#dim,* and *G,* or *Am7, Bm7, Cmaj7, D7, Em7, F#m7♭5,* and *Gmaj7.*

Our final six examples are extended, sequenced modal lines employing extreme legato phrasing—in other words, tons of hammer-ons and pull-offs with as few pick attacks as possible. Look closely and you'll discover a different fretboard scale pattern lurking within each sequence. Rhythmically, we're looking at alternating six- and five-note groupings within 16th-note sextuplets on each beat. Notice how the eighth-note "pauses" on beats *two* and *four* are always played with the 1st finger, as are beats *one* and *three.* Be sure to follow the picking-hand instructions closely—they're crucial to the execution of these lines.

Ex. 9 sets up our minor-mode speed-lick template with *A Aeolian,* or the *A* minor scale. Ex. 10 adapts the sequence to *A Dorian* by sharping all of the *F's,* while Ex. 11 recasts it as *A Phrygian* by flatting all *B's.* Similarly, Ex. 12 transposes the original line to *A* major (or *A* Ionian, if you prefer), and then converts it to *A Lydian* (Ex. 13) and *A Mixolydian* (Ex. 14). You'll know you've nailed these lines when those tuplets feel like they're just rolling off your fingers.

Ex. 1   Am7

Ex. 2   Am7

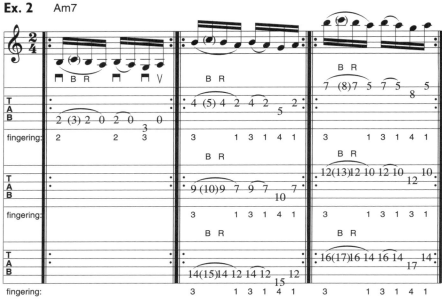

Ex. 3   Am7

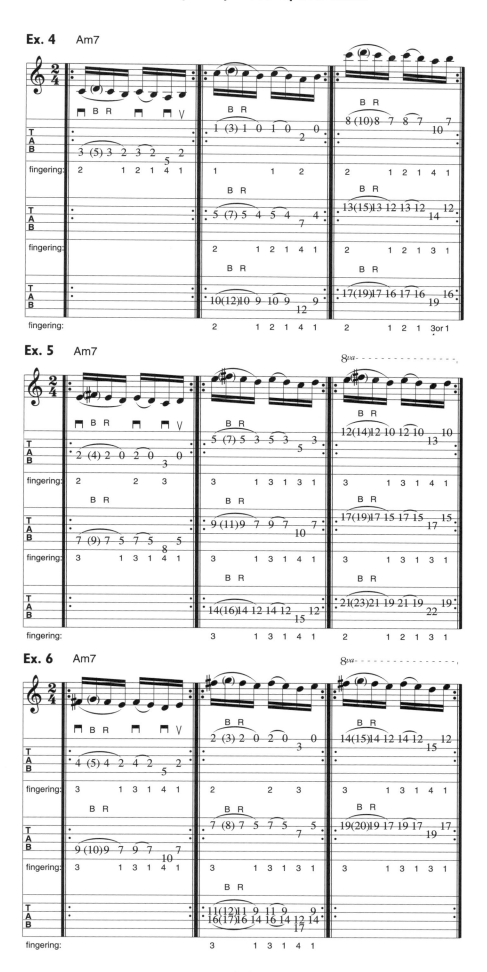

Ex. 7 Am7

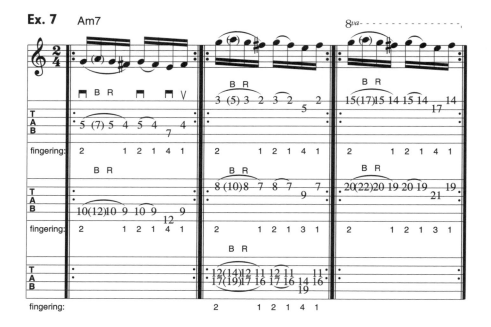

Ex. 8 Am7

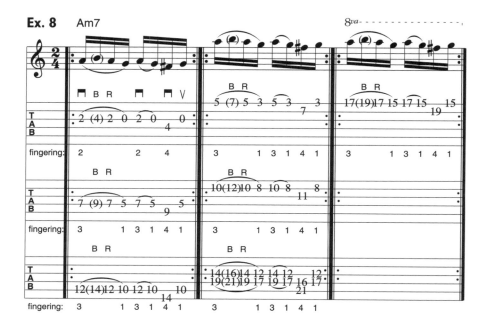

Ex. 9

A Aeolian

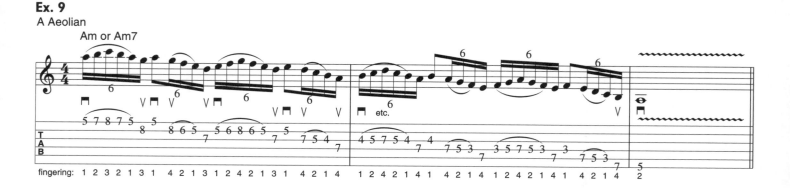

Ex. 10
A Dorian

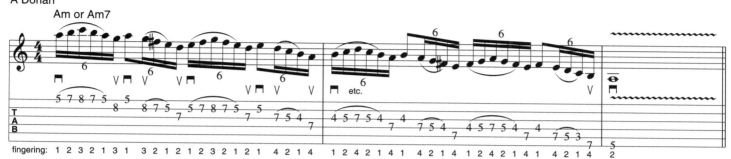

Ex. 11
A Phrygian

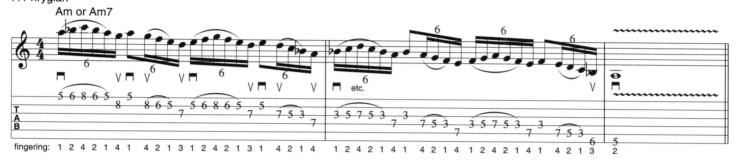

Ex. 12
A Major (Ionian)

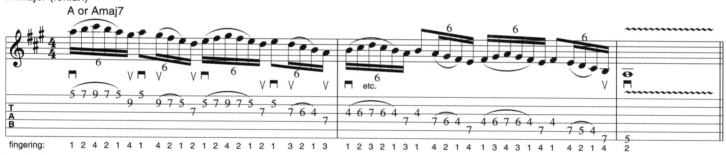

Ex. 13
A Lydian

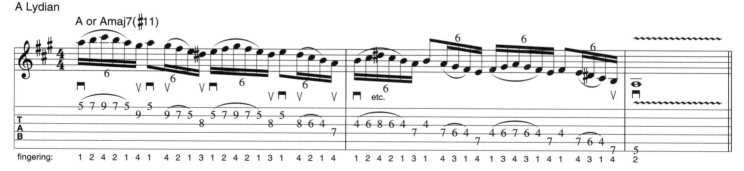

Ex. 14
A Mixolydian

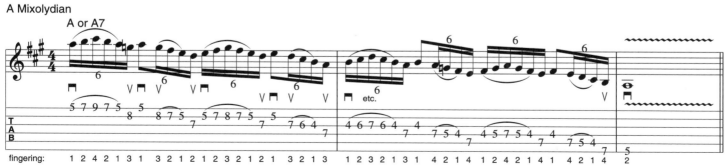

Nice work, but your Rock contract is up. The brass wants you to jump-start our new Jazz Lick Factory, so consider yourself transferred. But hey, you're still in the family!

JAZZ LICK FACTORY TOUR

The Jazz Lick Factory, our upstart division, consists of two facilities: One concentrates on swing and bebop, and the other specializes in smoky jazz-blues licks. Both offer a small but mighty line of four-note licks, which we balance with a healthy supply of ready-to-use one-bar licks and extended lines. Our goal is to make these licks accessible to adventurous blues and rock players who would like to inject jazz flavors into their solos while keeping the licks' hipness quotient high enough to interest seasoned jazz vets.

Of course, you can learn all of these licks by rote, but your benefits will increase in direct proportion to your knowledge of rhythm, major and minor scales (see page 60), and jazz harmony. (See *The Guitar Cookbook*.) Though our licks were designed to work with *Am7*, we've supplied a dozen ready-to-use chord voicings to illustrate all of the diatonic seventh chords relative to the key of *G*—where *Am7* resides as the IIm chord—plus a few altered *A♭7* and *B7* voicings. (See next page.) Be sure to explore how each lick functions with each chord. Technique-wise, slurring is the name of the game—slides, hammer-ons, and pull-offs abound, but string bends are totally absent. Most jazz players use moderately heavy-gauge strings with a wound *G*, though some prefer the darker sound of flatwounds. If you plan to play blues, rock, and jazz styles on the same instrument, you'll have to weigh the pros and cons of both light- and heavy-gauge strings.

Since we're planning to expand in the near future, we wanted to see what you could bring to the table. Play through these licks and lines, let us know how well they integrate with your existing musical vocabulary, and keep a list of things we could do better or more efficiently. The department heads will be in touch.

CHAPTER 15

FOUR-NOTE SWING AND BOP LICKS

Welcome to the swing and bop factory. The licks we produce here represent many of the same moves used by jazz greats from Charlie Christian to Mike Stern. Each one of our four-note swing/bop licks—notated in three octaves with multi-tab—is capable of spawning 24 (1x2x3x4) melodic permutations. As in blues and rock, this is a great way to get maximum melodic mileage out of any lick. Ex. 1 depicts a single four-note lick subjected to all 24 permutations, six starting on each note.

Due to the harmonic flexibility of the four-note licks in Examples 2–37, we've enhanced their Applications boxes with additional chord substitutions. Though these were initially designed as *Am7* licks, the boxes show how each one functions over every diatonic 7th chord in the key of *G* major: *Gmaj7* (I), *Am7* (IIm7), *Bm7* (IIIm7), *Cmaj7* (IVmaj7), *D7* (V7), *Em7* (VIm7), and *F#m7♭5* (VIIm7♭5); note that to save space in the boxes we've written only the Roman-numeral symbols for these chords. Additionally, each box includes two altered dominant 7th chords: *A♭7alt* (the ♭5 substitute for the V chord, *D7*), and *B7alt* (the V chord in *E* minor, the relative minor key of *G* major). Remember, it may become necessary to tack an appropriate chord tone onto the end of a lick to make it work for a particular application. (Astute users can also apply these subs to contemporary rock licks.)

We manufacture four licks starting on each note of the *A* Dorian mode (root–2–♭3–4–5–6–♭7, or *A–B–C–D–E–F#–G*). Integrated into these are four licks starting on the ♭5 (*E♭*, notated enharmonically as *D#*) from the *A* blues scale, and the 7 (*G#*) borrowed from the *A* harmonic minor scale.

You'll also notice that many of the slides, hammer-ons, and pull-offs in these licks occur between the "and" of beat *one* and the downbeat of beat *two*. This saxophone-influenced technique plays an important role in jazz phrasing.

If this more-advanced harmonic machinery is getting a little complicated, consult our recommended tech manual, *The Guitar Cookbook*.

Ex. 1

Six permutations starting on first note:

Six permutations starting on second note:

Six permutations starting on third note:

Six permutations starting on fourth note:

Ex. 2

Applications:				
Am7(II)	R	2	b3	4
D7(V)	5	6	b7	R
Gmaj7(I)	2	3	4	5
Cmaj7(IV)	6	7	R	9
Em7(VI)	4	5	b6	b7
F#m7b5(VII)	b3	4	b5	b6
Bm7(III)	b7	R	b2	b3
Ab7alt	b9	#9	3	b5
B7alt	b7	R	b9	#9

Ex. 3

Applications:				
Am7(II)	R	2	b3	5
D7(V)	5	6	b7	9
Gmaj7(I)	2	3	4	6
Cmaj7(IV)	6	7	R	3
Em7(VI)	4	5	b6	R
F#m7b5(VII)	b3	4	b5	b7
Bm7(III)	b7	R	b2	4
Ab7alt	b9	#9	3	#5
B7alt	b7	R	b9	11

Ex. 4

Applications:				
Am7(II)	R	2	b3	b7
D7(V)	5	6	b7	11
Gmaj7(I)	2	3	4	R
Cmaj7(IV)	6	7	R	5
Em7(VI)	4	5	b6	b3
F#m7b5(VII)	b3	4	b5	b9
Bm7(III)	b7	R	b2	b6
Ab7alt	b9	#9	3	7
B7alt	b7	R	b9	#5

Ex. 5

Applications:				
Am7(II)	R	b3	5	b7
D7(V)	5	b7	9	11
Gmaj7(I)	2	4	6	R
Cmaj7(IV)	6	R	3	5
Em7(VI)	4	b6	R	b3
F#m7b5(VII)	b3	b5	b7	b9
Bm7(III)	b7	b2	4	b6
Ab7alt	b9	3	#5	7
B7alt	b7	b9	11	b6

Ex. 6

Applications:				
Am7(II)	2	♭3	4	5
D7(V)	6	♭7	R	9
Gmaj7(I)	3	4	5	6
Cmaj7(IV)	7	R	9	3
Em7(VI)	5	♭6	♭7	R
F♯m7♭5(VII)	4	♭5	♭6	♭7
Bm7(III)	R	♭2	♭3	4
A♭7alt	♯9	3	♭5	♯5
B7alt	R	♭9	♯9	11

Ex. 7

Applications:				
Am7(II)	2	♭3	5	♭7
D7(V)	6	♭7	9	11
Gmaj7(I)	3	4	6	R
Cmaj7(IV)	7	R	3	5
Em7(VI)	5	♭6	R	♭3
F♯m7♭5(VII)	4	♭5	♭7	♭9
Bm7(III)	R	♭2	4	♭6
A♭7alt	♯9	3	♯5	7
B7alt	R	♭9	11	♭6

Ex. 8

Applications:				
Am7(II)	9	♭3	7	R
D7(V)	6	♭7	♯11	5
Gmaj7(I)	3	4	♭9	9
Cmaj7(IV)	7	R	♯5	6
Em7(VI)	5	♭6	3	4
F♯m7♭5(VII)	4	♭5	2	♭3
Bm7(III)	R	♭2	6	♭7
A♭7alt	♯9	3	R	♭9
B7alt	R	♭9	6	♭7

Ex. 9

Applications:				
Am7(II)	2	4	6	R
D7(V)	6	R	3	5
Gmaj7(I)	3	5	7	9
Cmaj7(IV)	7	9	♯11	13
Em7(VI)	5	♭7	9	4
F♯m7♭5(VII)	4	♭6	R	♭3
Bm7(III)	R	♭3	5	♭7
A♭7alt	♯9	♭5	♭7	♭9
B7alt	R	♯9	5	♭7

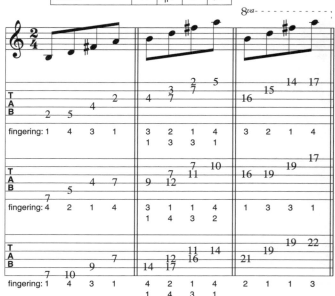

Ex. 10

Applications:				
Am7(II)	♭3	4	5	♭7
D7(V)	♭7	R	9	11
Gmaj7(I)	4	5	6	R
Cmaj7(IV)	R	2	3	5
Em7(VI)	♭6	♭7	R	♭3
F♯m7♭5(VII)	♭5	♭6	♭7	♭9
Bm7(III)	♭2	♭3	4	♭6
A♭7alt	3	♭5	♯5	7
B7alt	♭9	♯9	11	♯5

Ex. 11

Applications:				
Am7(II)	♭3	5	6	R
D7(V)	♭7	9	3	5
Gmaj7(I)	4	6	7	9
Cmaj7(IV)	R	3	♯11	6
Em7(VI)	♭6	R	9	4
F♯m7♭5(VII)	♭5	♭7	R	♭3
Bm7(III)	♭2	4	5	♭7
A♭7alt	3	♯5	♭7	♭9
B7alt	♭9	11	5	♭7

Ex. 12

Applications:				
Am7(II)	♭3	5	6	9
D7(V)	♭7	9	3	6
Gmaj7(I)	4	6	7	3
Cmaj7(IV)	R	3	♯11	7
Em7(VI)	♭6	R	9	5
F♯m7♭5(VII)	♭5	♭7	R	4
Bm7(III)	♭2	4	5	R
A♭7alt	3	♯5	♭7	♯9
B7alt	♭9	11	5	R

Ex. 13

Applications:				
Am7(II)	♭3	5	♭7	9
D7(V)	♭7	9	11	13
Gmaj7(I)	4	6	R	3
Cmaj7(IV)	R	3	5	7
Em7(VI)	♭6	R	♭3	5
F♯m7♭5(VII)	♭5	♭7	♭9	4
Bm7(III)	♭2	4	♭6	R
A♭7alt	3	♯5	7	♯9
B7alt	♭9	11	♯5	R

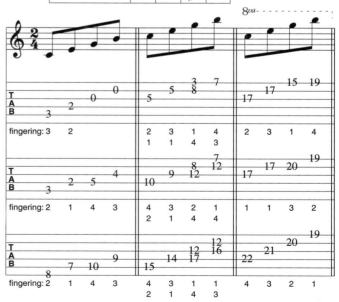

Ex. 14

Applications:				
Am7(II)	4	3	♭3	5
D7(V)	R	7	♭7	9
Gmaj7(I)	5	♭5	4	6
Cmaj7(IV)	9	♭9	R	3
Em7(VI)	♭7	6	♭6	R
F♯m7♭5(VII)	♭6	5	♭5	♭7
Bm7(III)	♭3	2	♭2	4
A♭7alt	♭5	4	3	♯5
B7alt	♯9	9	♭9	11

Ex. 15

Applications:				
Am7(II)	4	3	♭3	5
D7(V)	R	7	♭7	2
Gmaj7(I)	5	♭5	4	6
Cmaj7(IV)	9	♭9	R	3
Em7(VI)	♭7	6	♭6	R
F♯m7♭5(VII)	♭6	5	♭5	♭7
Bm7(III)	♭3	2	♭2	4
A♭7alt	♭5	4	3	♯5
B7alt	♯9	9	♭9	11

Ex. 16

Applications:				
Am7(II)	4	♭7	6	R
D7(V)	R	4	3	5
Gmaj7(I)	5	R	7	9
Cmaj7(IV)	2	5	♯11	6
Em7(VI)	♭7	♭3	9	11
F♯m7♭5(VII)	♭6	♭9	R	♭3
Bm7(III)	♭3	♭6	5	♭7
A♭7alt	♭5	7	♭7	♭9
B7alt	♯9	♯5	5	♭7

Ex. 17

Applications:				
Am7(II)	4	6	R	♭3
D7(V)	R	3	5	♭7
Gmaj7(I)	5	7	9	11
Cmaj7(IV)	2	♯11	6	R
Em7(VI)	♭7	9	11	♭6
F♯m7♭5(VII)	♭6	R	♭3	♭5
Bm7(III)	♭3	5	♭7	♭2
A♭7alt	♭5	♭7	♭9	3
B7alt	♯9	5	♭7	♭9

Ex. 18

Applications:				
Am7(II)	b5	5	6	b7
D7(V)	b9	9	3	11
Gmaj7(I)	#5	6	7	R
Cmaj7(IV)	b3	3	b5	5
Em7(VI)	7	R	9	b3
F#m7b5(VII)	6	b7	R	b9
Bm7(III)	3	4	5	b6
Ab7alt	5	#5	b7	7
B7alt	3	11	5	#5

Ex. 19

Applications:				
Am7(II)	b5	5	b7	R
D7(V)	b9	9	11	5
Gmaj7(I)	#5	6	R	9
Cmaj7(IV)	b3	3	5	6
Em7(VI)	7	R	b3	4
F#m7b5(VII)	6	b7	b9	b3
Bm7(III)	3	4	b6	b7
Ab7alt	5	#5	7	b9
B7alt	3	11	#5	b7

Ex. 20

Applications:				
Am7(II)	b5	5	b7	9
D7(V)	b9	9	11	6
Gmaj7(I)	#5	6	R	3
Cmaj7(IV)	b3	3	5	7
Em7(VI)	7	R	b3	5
F#m7b5(VII)	6	b7	b9	4
Bm7(III)	3	4	b6	R
Ab7alt	5	#5	7	#9
B7alt	3	11	#5	R

Ex. 21

Applications:				
Am7(II)	b5	5	b7	b3
D7(V)	b9	9	11	b7
Gmaj7(I)	#5	6	R	4
Cmaj7(IV)	b3	3	5	R
Em7(VI)	7	R	b3	b6
F#m7b5(VII)	6	b7	b9	b5
Bm7(III)	3	4	b6	b2
Ab7alt	5	#5	7	3
B7alt	3	11	#5	b9

Ex. 22

Applications:				
Am7(II)	5	6	♭7	R
D7(V)	9	3	11	5
Gmaj7(I)	6	7	R	9
Cmaj7(IV)	3	♭5	5	6
Em7(VI)	R	9	♭3	11
F♯m7♭5(VII)	♭7	R	♭9	♭3
Bm7(III)	4	5	♭6	♭7
A♭7alt	♯5	♭7	7	♭9
B7alt	11	5	♯5	♭7

Ex. 23

Applications:				
Am7(II)	5	6	♭7	♭3
D7(V)	9	3	11	♭7
Gmaj7(I)	6	7	R	4
Cmaj7(IV)	3	♭5	5	R
Em7(VI)	R	9	♭3	♭6
F♯m7♭5(VII)	♭7	R	♭9	♭5
Bm7(III)	4	5	♭6	♭2
A♭7alt	♯5	♭7	7	3
B7alt	11	5	♯5	♭9

Ex. 24

Applications:				
Am7(II)	5	R	2	♭3
D7(V)	9	5	6	♭7
Gmaj7(I)	6	9	3	4
Cmaj7(IV)	3	6	7	R
Em7(VI)	R	11	5	♭6
F♯m7♭5(VII)	♭7	♭3	4	♭5
Bm7(III)	4	♭7	R	♭2
A♭7alt	♯5	♭9	♯9	3
B7alt	11	♭7	R	♭9

Ex. 25

Applications:				
Am7(II)	5	♭7	9	11
D7(V)	9	11	13	R
Gmaj7(I)	6	R	3	5
Cmaj7(IV)	3	5	7	9
Em7(VI)	R	♭3	5	♭7
F♯m7♭5(VII)	♭7	♭9	4	♭6
Bm7(III)	4	♭6	R	♭3
A♭7alt	♯5	7	♯9	♭5
B7alt	11	♯5	R	♯9

Ex. 26

Applications:				
Am7(II)	6	♭7	R	9
D7(V)	3	11	5	13
Gmaj7(I)	7	R	2	3
Cmaj7(IV)	♭5	5	6	7
Em7(VI)	9	♭3	11	5
F♯m7♭5(VII)	R	♭9	♭3	4
Bm7(III)	5	♭6	♭7	R
A♭7alt	♭7	7	♭9	♯9
B7alt	5	♯5	♭7	R

Ex. 27

Applications:				
Am7(II)	6	♭7	R	♭3
D7(V)	3	4	5	♭7
Gmaj7(I)	7	R	2	4
Cmaj7(IV)	♭5	5	6	R
Em7(VI)	9	♭3	11	♭6
F♯m7♭5(VII)	R	♭9	♭3	♭5
Bm7(III)	5	♭6	♭7	♭2
A♭7alt	♭7	7	♭9	3
B7alt	5	♯5	♭7	♭9

Ex. 28

Applications:				
Am7(II)	6	♭7	9	4
D7(V)	3	4	6	R
Gmaj7(I)	7	R	3	5
Cmaj7(IV)	♭5	5	7	9
Em7(VI)	9	♭3	5	♭7
F♯m7♭5(VII)	R	♭9	4	♭6
Bm7(III)	5	♭6	R	♭3
A♭7alt	♭	7	♯9	♭5
B7alt	5	♯5	R	♯9

Ex. 29

Applications:				
Am7(II)	6	R	♭3	5
D7(V)	3	5	♭7	9
Gmaj7(I)	7	2	4	6
Cmaj7(IV)	♭5	6	R	3
Em7(VI)	9	11	♭6	R
F♯m7♭5(VII)	R	♭3	♭5	♭7
Bm7(III)	5	♭7	♭2	4
A♭7alt	♭7	♭9	3	♯5
B7alt	5	♭7	♭9	11

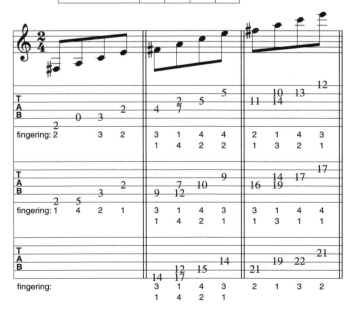

Ex. 30

Applications:				
Am7(II)	♭7	R	2	♭3
D7(V)	4	5	6	♭7
Gmaj7(I)	R	2	3	4
Cmaj7(IV)	5	6	7	R
Em7(VI)	♭3	4	5	♭6
F#m7♭5(VII)	♭9	♭3	4	♭5
Bm7(III)	♭6	♭7	R	♭2
A♭7alt	7	♭9	#9	3
B7alt	#5	♭7	R	♭9

Ex. 31

Applications:				
Am7(II)	♭7	7	R	♭3
D7(V)	4	♭5	5	♭7
Gmaj7(I)	R	♭2	2	4
Cmaj7(IV)	5	#5	6	R
Em7(VI)	♭3	3	4	♭6
F#m7♭5(VII)	♭2	2	♭3	♭5
Bm7(III)	♭6	6	♭7	♭2
A♭7alt	7	R	♭9	3
B7alt	#5	6	♭7	♭9

Ex. 32

Applications:				
Am7(II)	♭7	R	♭3	5
D7(V)	4	5	♭7	9
Gmaj7(I)	R	2	4	6
Cmaj7(IV)	5	6	R	3
Em7(VI)	♭3	4	♭6	R
F#m7♭5(VII)	♭9	♭3	♭5	♭7
Bm7(III)	♭6	♭7	♭2	4
A♭7alt	7	♭9	3	#5
B7alt	#5	♭7	♭9	11

Ex. 33

Applications:				
Am7(II)	♭7	2	4	6
D7(V)	4	6	R	3
Gmaj7(I)	R	3	5	7
Cmaj7(IV)	5	7	9	#11
Em7(VI)	♭3	5	♭7	9
F#m7♭5(VII)	♭9	4	♭6	R
Bm7(III)	♭6	R	♭3	5
A♭7alt	7	#9	♭5	♭7
B7alt	#5	R	#9	5

Ex. 34

Applications:				
Am7(II)	7	R	2	♭3
D7(V)	♭5	5	6	♭7
Gmaj7(I)	♭2	2	3	4
Cmaj7(IV)	#5	6	7	R
Em7(VI)	3	4	5	♭6
F#m7♭5(VII)	2	♭3	4	♭5
Bm7(III)	6	♭7	R	♭2
A♭7alt	R	♭9	#9	3
B7alt	6	♭7	R	♭9

Ex. 35

Applications:				
Am7(II)	7	R	5	♭3
D7(V)	♭5	5	2	♭7
Gmaj7(I)	♭2	2	6	4
Cmaj7(IV)	#5	6	3	R
Em7(VI)	3	4	R	♭6
F#m7♭5(VII)	2	♭3	♭7	♭5
Bm7(III)	6	♭7	4	♭2
A♭7alt	R	♭9	#5	3
B7alt	6	♭7	11	♭9

Ex. 36

Applications:				
Am7(II)	7	R	♭3	5
D7(V)	♭5	5	♭7	2
Gmaj7(I)	♭2	2	4	6
Cmaj7(IV)	#5	6	R	3
Em7(VI)	3	4	♭6	R
F#m7♭5(VII)	2	♭3	♭5	♭7
Bm7(III)	6	♭7	♭2	4
A♭7alt	R	♭9	3	#5
B7alt	6	♭7	♭9	11

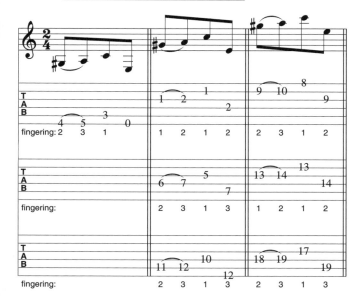

Ex. 37

Applications:				
Am7(II)	7	R	♭3	5
D7(V)	♭5	5	♭7	9
Gmaj7(I)	♭2	2	4	6
Cmaj7(IV)	#5	6	R	3
Em7(VI)	3	4	♭6	R
F#m7♭5(VII)	2	♭3	♭5	♭7
Bm7(III)	6	♭7	♭2	4
A♭7alt	R	♭9	3	#5
B7alt	6	♭7	♭9	11

CHAPTER 16

ONE-BAR SWING AND BOP LICKS

Many of the one-bar swing and bop licks illustrated in Examples 1–20 (sans Apps boxes and multi-octaves) were conceived by combining pairs of four-note licks. As you work through the first 20 examples, you'll notice that the licks begin on various A Dorian scale tones (root- 2–♭3–4–5–6–♭7), plus a 7 borrowed from the A harmonic minor scale.

These A Dorian–based II-chord licks also work well with any of the chord substitutions contained in the Applications boxes for the previous four-note licks. Again, you may have to add a final target tone to fit the chord of the moment.

Examples 21–26 show you how to attach a target chord tone or other extension to the end of a one-bar A minor lick. You can alter this target tone to comply with any chord in the previous Apps boxes.

Examples 27–32 include a two- or three-note pickup to each one-bar A minor lick. Some of these licks also feature tacked-on target tones.

You can approximate saxophone-like phrasing—a very desirable trait for a jazz guitarist—by incorporating sweep-picked and hammered-and-pulled eighth-note triplets into a lick. Examples 33–35 illustrate three ways to apply sax-y phrasing techniques to a given lick. Adapt these to as many of the previous one-bar licks as possible.

Ex. 1–4

Ex. 5–8

Ex. 9–12

Ex. 13–16

Ex. 17–20

Ex. 21–23

Ex. 24–26

Ex. 27–28

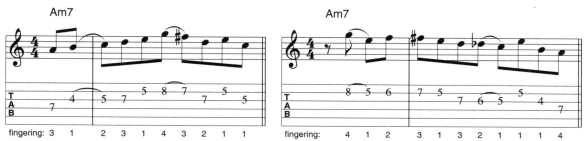

Ex. 29–30

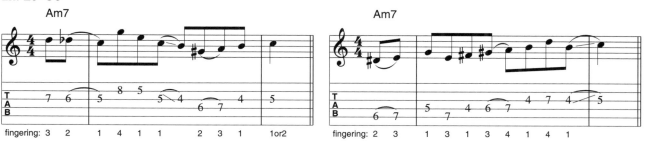

Ex. 31–32

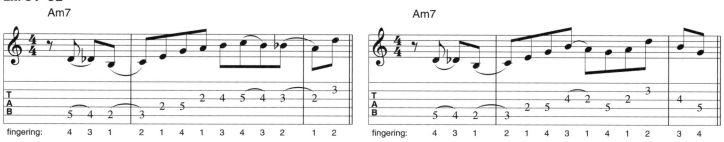

Ex. 33

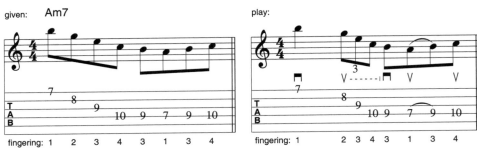

Ex. 34

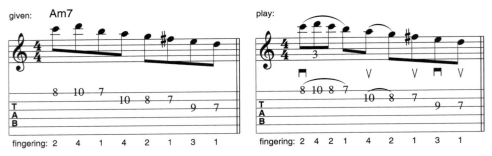

Ex. 35

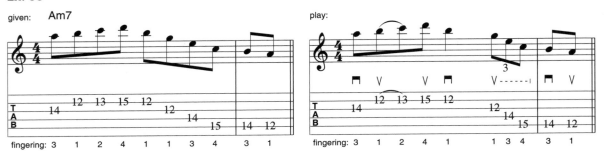

FOUR-NOTE JAZZ-BLUES LICKS

You may feel a bit of déjà vu as you dig into the following four-note jazz-blues licks. In essence, we've come full circle; this facility uses exactly the same raw materials as the Blues Lick Factory—namely, the *A* blues scale.

We've built two dozen licks—four starting on each step of the *A* blues scale (root–♭3–4–♭5–5–♭7)—and notated them in three octaves with multi-tab (Examples 1–24). Users can apply them to *Am7* or a variety of *A7* colors, including *A9*, *A13*, and *A7♯9*. Again, the bending so prevalent in blues has been replaced with slippery slides, hammer-ons, and pull-offs.

Examples 25–34 walk you through ten subtle variations of a sultry jazz-blues lick. The two-note diads and smoky hammer/pull moves lend a Hammond-organ vibe to the proceedings.

Ex. 1

Am7 or A7♯9

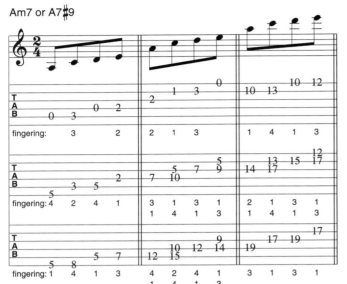

Ex. 2

Am7 or A7♯9

Ex. 3

Am7 or A7♯9

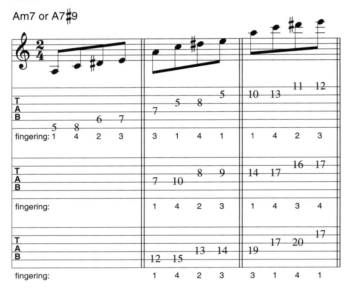

Ex. 4

Am7 or A7♯9

Ex. 5

Am7 or A7♯9

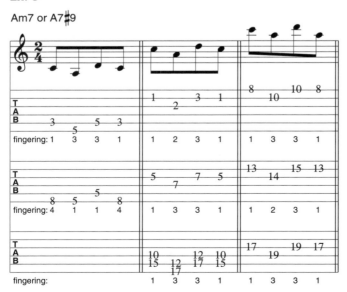

Ex. 6

Am7 or A7♯9

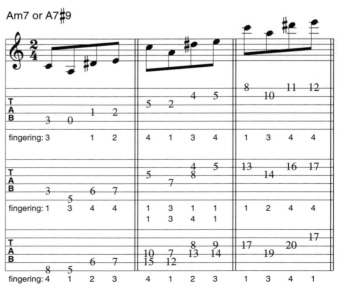

Ex. 7

Am7 or A7#9

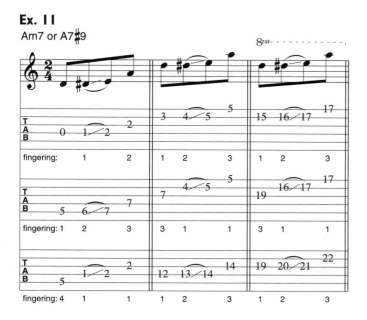

Ex. 8

Am7 or A7#9

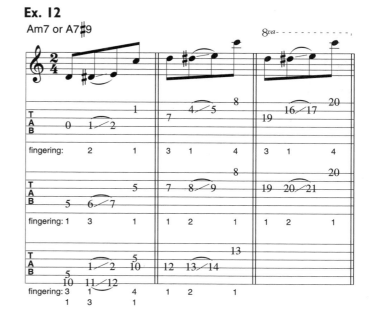

Ex. 9

Am7 or A7#9

Ex. 10

Am7 or A7#9

Ex. 11

Am7 or A7#9

Ex. 12

Am7 or A7#9

Ex. 13
Am7 or A7#9

Ex. 15
Am7 or A7#9

Ex. 17
Am7 or A7#9

Ex. 14
Am7 or A7#9

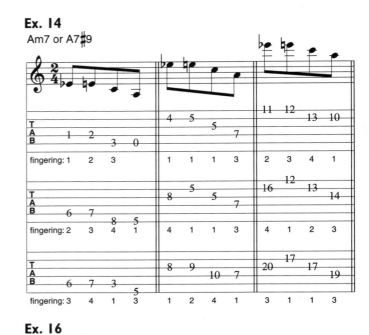

Ex. 16
Am7 or A7#9

Ex. 18
Am7 or A7#9

Ex. 19
Am7 or A7#9

Ex. 21
Am7 or A7#9

Ex. 23
Am7 or A7#9

Ex. 20
Am7 or A7#9

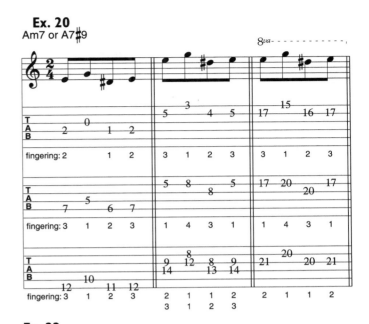

Ex. 22
Am7 or A7#9

Ex. 24
Am7 or A7#9

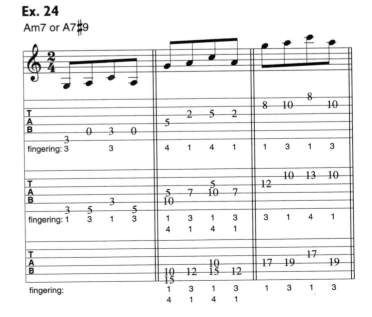

Ex. 25
Am7 or A7#9

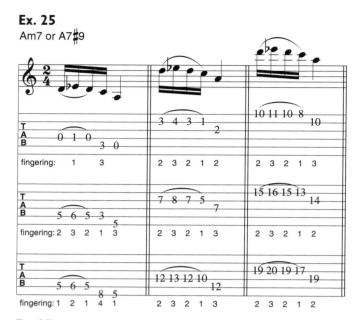

Ex. 27
Am7 or A7#9

Ex. 29
Am7 or A7#9

Ex. 26
Am7 or A7#9

Ex. 28
Am7 or A7#9

Ex. 30
Am7 or A7#9

Ex. 31
Am7 or A7#9

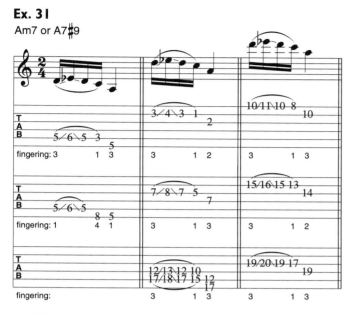

Ex. 32
Am7 or A7#9

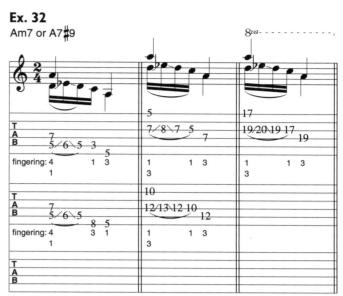

Ex. 33
Am7 or A7#9

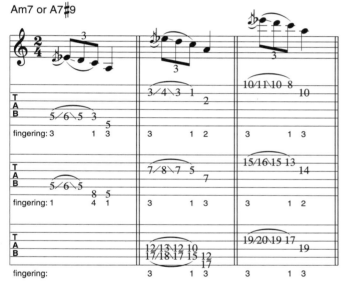

Ex. 34
Am7 or A7#9

CHAPTER 18

EXTENDED JAZZ-BLUES LINES

Our top-of-the-line elite fleet at the Jazz Lick Factory gathers 13 smoky lines in the styles of Kenny Burrell, Grant Green, George Benson, and other jazz-blues greats (Examples 1–13). These extended lines range from two to four bars in length and come ready to drop into your next *A* minor blues excursion.

Minor blues progressions share the common 12-bar blues form, but the I and IV chords are minor 7ths instead of dominant 7ths. A typical *A* minor blues progression looks like this, bar by bar: *Am7/Am7/Am7/Am7/Dm7/Dm7/Am7/Am7/Bm7♭5/E7alt/ Am7/Am7*. Try fitting the *Am7* lines into bars 1, 2, 3, 4, 7, 8, 11, and 12, and the *Dm7* lines into bars 5 and 6.

Some of our jazz-blues lines are tailor-made for specific parts of an *A* minor blues progression. Ex. 12 is perfect for navigating the IVm–Im (*Dm7–Am7*) change in bars 5–8, while Ex. 13 was designed to cover the IIm7♭5–V7–Im (*Bm7♭5–E7alt–Am7*) turnaround in bars 9–12.

It doesn't get any more authentic than this. Pull out a few of these moves on the bandstand and watch the heads turn. You can pair these lines in the same way you combined four-note and one-bar licks. For instance, try tagging Ex. 6 to the end of Ex. 1. Cool, eh? See how many combinations you can concoct.

Ex. 1

Ex. 2

Ex. 3

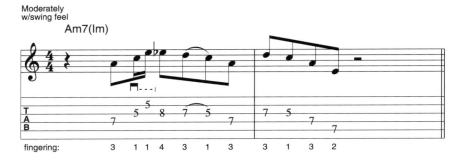

Ex. 4

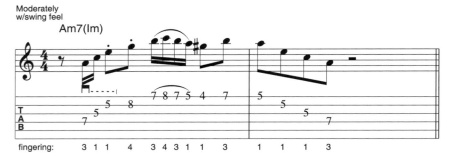

Ex. 5

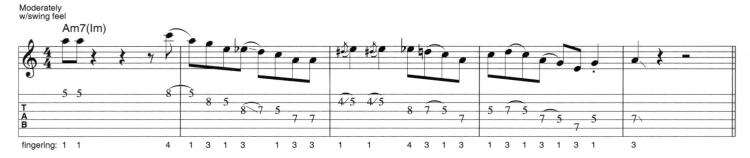

Ex. 6

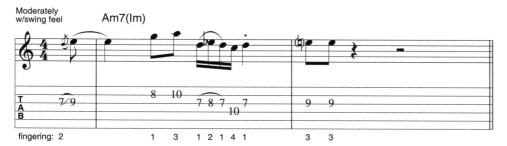

Ex. 7

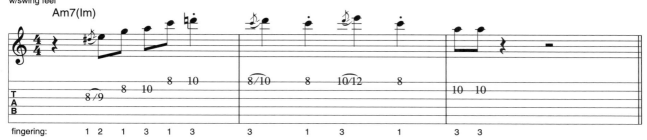

Ex. 8

Ex. 9

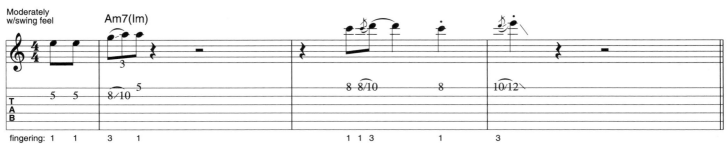

Ex. 10

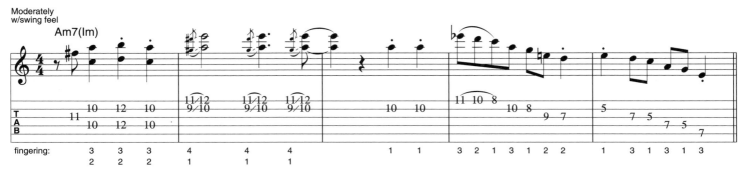

Ex. 11

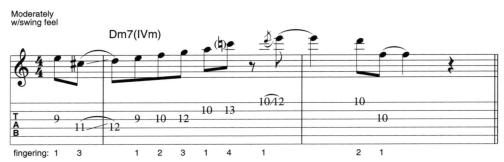

Ex. 12

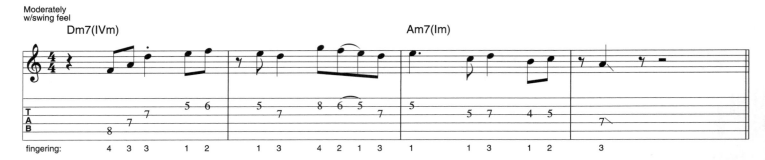

Ex. 13

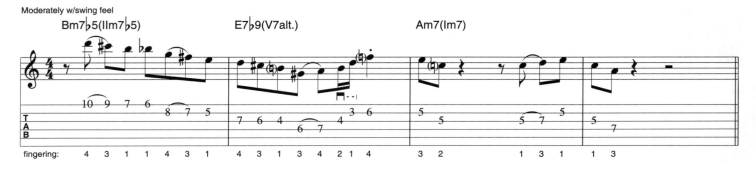

Great work, boss! You've really done wonders with this place. But I've got some bad news; you've been laid off. Budget cuts, you know? But don't worry; you're still in the family—now go get a job playing the guitar!

WHEN IT COMES TO GUITARS, WE WROTE THE BOOK.

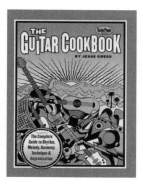
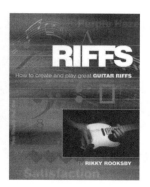
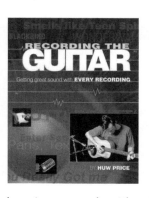

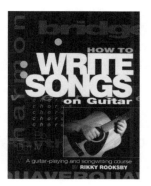